T0129372

the miracle of

MERCY

Filling the World with the Love of God

the *miracle* of MERCY

Terry Rush

HOWARD®
PUBLISHING CO.

The Miracle of Mercy © 1999 by Terry Rush
All rights reserved. Printed in the United States of America
Published by Howard Publishing Co., Inc.,
3117 North 7th Street, West Monroe, Louisiana 71291-2227

99 00 01 02 03 04 05 06 07 08   10 9 8 7 6 5 4 3 2 1

Library of Congress Cataloging-in-Publication Data

Rush, Terry.
    The miracle of mercy : filling the world with the love of God /
Terry Rush.
       p. cm.
    Includes bibliographical references.
    ISBN 978-1-58229-010-2
    1. Mercy. I. Title.
BV4647.M4R88   1999
241'.4—dc21   99-19367
                                                 CIP

Edited by Philis Boultinghouse
Interior design by LinDee Loveland

*Dedicated to the memory of
Curt Flood*

When I was a young boy, Curt Flood served as both my idol and hero. His skill on the baseball field was inspiring to wide-eyed dreamers who saw themselves one day duplicating his quick, fine-tuned talent . . . awing everyone in the stadium.

In later years Curt became my friend and brother. He was more than a baseball star. He was a man who, although often betrayed, misunderstood, and misrepresented, continued to show mercy, courtesy, and love. He refused to waste his latter years in bitterness. Rather, he displayed his true champion-heart. He lived focused on things that mattered. He chose to trade suspicion for hope and disappointments of the past for the joy of the present.

Curt knew how to do battle. He found victory, even in apparent losses, because he wasn't selfish. He had a fire for the well-being of his fellow man. To the very end, he never let that blaze die down. I miss him . . . so much.

CONTENTS

ACKNOWLEDGMENTS . . . *ix*

ONE
the marvel of MERCY . . . *1*

TWO
the mystery of MERCY . . . *11*

THREE
the mandate of MERCY . . . *25*

FOUR
the meaning of MERCY . . . *39*

FIVE
the master of MERCY . . . *53*

SIX
the menace of MERCY . . . *67*

CONTENTS

SEVEN

the miracle of MERCY ... *81*

EIGHT

the might of MERCY ... *101*

NINE

the measure of MERCY ... *115*

TEN

the methods of MERCY ... *133*

ELEVEN

the misgivings of MERCY ... *149*

TWELVE

the message of MERCY ... *167*

NOTES ... *185*

ACKNOWLEDGMENTS

Philip Yancey gave me his input for an entire day as to whether this concept was worthy of continued investigation. His notes of encouragement filtering in over the fax machine kept me in the search. Doug Ferguson and Linda Jones read tattered, incomplete thoughts and offered desperately needed, well-advised insight. Then, Philis Boultinghouse's heart for this material gave this book its completed and, I think, fertile capacity to give new birth to dying hearts. Thanks to all the crew at Howard Publishing for presenting to the reading community a treatise that will plow deeply into the fields of reconciliation and recovery.

the marvel of MERCY

CHAPTER 1

Praise be to the God and Father of our Lord Jesus Christ! In his great mercy he has given us new birth into a living hope through the resurrection of Jesus Christ from the dead.

—1 Peter 1:3

1

the marvel of MERCY

Mary Karr, in her memoir *The Liar's Club*, tells of a Texas uncle who, after a fight with his wife, remained married to her yet did not speak to her for forty years. He thought she spent too much money on sugar. He sawed their house down the middle and moved his half several yards away.[1] He gave new meaning to the term *halfway house*.

Upon telling this story, Philip Yancey points out,

> Forgiveness offers a way out. It does not settle all questions . . . but it does allow a relationship to start over, to begin anew. In that way, said Solzhenitsyn, we differ from all animals. Not our capacity to

think, but our capacity to repent and to forgive makes us different. Only humans can perform that most unnatural act, which transcends the relentless law of nature.

Now note his counsel: "If we do not transcend nature, we remain bound to 'the people we cannot forgive, held in their vise grip."[2] The man sawed the house in half! Over money spent on sugar! This shows the desperate efforts of some to retaliate, to do harm. But in reality, the greatest harm was to himself. We must change this dominant spiritual gene found in each of us.

A World without Mercy

America's condition is not declining simply because violence, greed, and immorality moved in but because forgiveness, grace, and mercy moved out. Her churches are not dwindling because they lack the creative juices to effectively market their cause. It's because we have been just as indignant as the world we are trying to save. We have failed the call of Jesus to love our enemies as we do our friends. Stinging words and snobbish attitudes have driven the masses from the house of God to live on the streets of a cold and loveless world.

Harsh and stubborn responses have deterred many a softening heart from giving in and making up. Pride refuses to say the simplest things like, "I'm sorry" or "Please, would you forgive me?" or "I was wrong." Independence has convinced us, at times, that we need no one. We do think we are better off as islands.

Indeed, many have made concerted efforts to make a difference for good. Money has been contributed. Foundations have been forged. Humanitarianism is abundant and deserves our applause and participation. Yet, tension increases, privacy fences abound, and individualism holds potential apologies and reunions at bay.

The Choice to Be Merciful

Yet, there is hope. For all the isolation of the information age, it does offer vast choices. Everywhere, from automobiles to cereals to deodorants, choice is abundant. It's up to me to decide how I will respond to the wars raging within and without me. *I* choose. And oftentimes, choice is based on what I *believe* about the circumstances in my life. William Backus and Marie Chapian wrote in *Telling Yourself the Truth*, "In emotional and mental health, what you believe is *all important*. . . . Other people, circumstances, events and material things are *not* what make you happy.

What you *believe* about these things is what makes you happy or unhappy."[3] Those three sentences changed my life. Whether or not I live a life of forgiveness, compassion, and mercy is up to me and no one else. I decide.

And some people are choosing the road less traveled. A global warming is taking place in the hearts of many. Reports of mended relationships, unearthly forgiveness, and surprising compassion are met with rave reviews. Talk shows and news reports gladly tell of victims who walk a higher road by refusing to hold on to bitterness and anger toward personal offenders. Many believers are tired of being mean. Preachers are tired of being loud and abrasive. The blessings that result are divine.

Stanley Hauerwas and William Willimon were on to something when they wrote, "Our everyday experience of life in the congregation is training in the arts of forgiveness; it is everyday, practical confirmation of the truthfulness of the Christian vision."[4] Great hope is found in the determination to "train in the art of forgiveness."

Training does not come from reading good books, however. It comes by being offended. This calls us to a kingdom style that not only works but also *is work*. It's one thing to talk the talk in Sunday school with lifeless flannel graph. It's another to walk the talk when a drunk runs over your son. The former requires nothing more than religious chatter. The latter exists only in a newly created person and originates in undaunted courage to love one so irresponsible. It calls for strength of character—other worldly strength. It calls for a characteristic that few dare to grapple with. It calls for the marvel of mercy.

The Marvel of Mercy

Mercy is what God is about. And it's what we are to be about. The marvel of mercy lived out in everyday lives is every bit as powerful as a nuclear warhead. Even more so. But be warned. Mercy's calling and demands may at times seem beyond reason. Don't sweat it. So is a nuclear warhead. But along with mercy's high calling, God issues us the unequaled power required to live it out.

William Willimon tells a marvelous story about a college student ministering in the inner city of Philadelphia for a summer. Following is a paraphrase of that story:

The greenhorn hesitantly made his way off of the bus and onto the sidewalk of one of the worst looking housing projects in town. As he entered the huge, dark tenement he was first greeted by a horrible odor. Windows were out. No lights in the hall. He heard a baby crying and skeptically knocked on the door.

A woman holding a naked baby opened the door slightly. Disgruntled, she wanted to know what he wanted. "I'm here to tell you about Jesus." She cursed him all the way down the hall, down the steps, and out to the sidewalk.

The boy sat on the curb and cried.

Upon noticing a store on the corner, he recalled the baby had no diapers and that the woman was smoking. He bought a box of disposable diapers and a pack of cigarettes. With fierce trepidation the student made another trek up that memorable flight of stairs. Upon hearing the knock, the ill-tempered woman opened the door. He slid the box and the cigarettes across the threshold. She said, "Come in," and then sternly, "Sit down."

He fitted a diaper on the baby and, although he didn't smoke, did have a cigarette with her when she offered one. Eventually she asked what a nice boy like him was doing in a place like that. He told her everything he knew about Jesus . . . in about five minutes.

He later reported to his colleagues, "I not only got to tell 'em about Jesus, I met Jesus. I went out to save somebody, and I ended up getting saved. I became a disciple.[5]

Along with this naive college student, we can share in the marvel of mercy—but only if we are willing to be involved in a most radical process. The cadence of mercy does not move to the rhythm of mediocrity. It can't, for it assumes we are in trouble. Mercy is the cure for injury. It does what we can't, and it's tough too. Mercy is not about the trivial. It's about the unlikely and the impossible. Mercy will not hedge on the truth. It will not hear of playing politics. Its public relations firm consists only of an innocent Nazarene, who was willing to take on the guilt of the guilty by being suspended from a cross in enormous humiliation. That's the marvel of mercy.

Answering the call of mercy is more than noble; it's appealing. It's enticing to all who are weary of giving it their best shot only to end up with broken hearts and shattered dreams. We are fatigued from trying to repair one-sided relationships and lopsided goals. The worries, the discouragements, the anxieties . . . where can we go?

Hope for the Weary

If you find yourself embroiled in a domestic war—the sort that is every bit as intense as the Mideast conflict—you will like this book. If you are tired of living out bitterness, animosity, avoidance, hostility, and even cruel hatred, you hold in your hand artillery for fresh hope. If you're worn down over family or career conflict, take heart.

The goal of this book is to offer empty souls a brave and daring hope. If your mind continually rehearses wounds and injuries, get ready. You are about to become aware of one of the most outrageous, most scandalous, most improbable, impossible facets of God—mercy.

Brennan Manning declares the power of the message of God to crack open our world.

> When the Gospel is preached with purity and power, it should force us to reassess the entire direction of our lives. The Word breaks our train of thought, cracks open our capsuled doctrine, shatters our life of comfortable piety and well-fed virtue. The flashing spirit of Jesus breaks new paths everywhere. The Gospel is no Pollyanna tale for the neutral but a cutting knife, rolling thunder, convulsive earthquake in the world of the human spirit.[6]

May the knife be sharpened, may the thunder clap, may the earthquake rumble! May the marvel of mercy break our train of thought . . . that a miracle might capture our hearts once again.

the *mystery* of MERCY

CHAPTER 2

For God has shut up all in disobedience that He might show mercy to all. Oh, the depth of the riches both of the wisdom and knowledge of God! How unsearchable are His judgments and unfathomable His ways!
—Romans 11:32–33 NASB

2

the mystery of MERCY

Is it possible in our land of computerized technology and space-age engineering to be amazed? Haven't we just about captured the imagination? The been-there-done-that crowd yawns with indifference. The technological and scientific progress of our time fills humankind with the notion that there is no more mystery to be revealed. I can see how unbelievers might be bored with God.

But how dare disciples of the Creator be bored? You gotta be kidding! Just look around! The wonders of the earth are beyond explanation. At the mere word of God, mountains range, oceans wave, time marches, chickens cluck, and the sun shines. And each of these wonders is for our enjoyment—not our explanation. Who cares about understanding it? We love it! We want more of it. We pay big bucks to take our families on two-week vacations to soak in the sensations of nature. And that's just the wonders of the physical realm!

What about the wonders of the spiritual realm? They are even more spectacular! Concepts like holiness, eternity, grace, forgiveness, new birth, eyes of the heart, justification, and transformation are exciting and warrant a passionate response! God is not dull! The life he gives is not ho-hum!

And what of mercy? It is truly one of God's most wonderful mysteries. It is too good to be true! This invisible and holy ointment of mercy penetrates society, replacing hurt and despair with hope and happiness. It binds the wounds of the oppressed, even when we don't know them—for strangers are often at our mercy.

Practicing mercy should fill our hearts with enthusiasm because it is a virtue of God. But we often reject it because we can't predict how it will all wash out. That is precisely why mercy is so mysterious. As imaginative as they may be, neither Disney nor Fox nor the summer Olympics can dazzle the mind the way God can. This chapter will not attempt to explain the riddle of God's incomprehensible mercy; rather it will call for your participation in it. Partake even when you don't understand. After all, isn't that our philosophy when we go to Six Flags?

Mercy Is Better Described Than Explained

William Willimon, in his book *The Intrusive Word,* proposes that "preachers are too eager to make sure that everyone understands, that everyone gets it. This inevitably means that too much of the obvious is explained, and too little of the mysterious is described."[1] I fear we may have discussed some biblical topics so often and so long that we feel we have a grip on them.

Have our endless repetitions tamed and domesticated Bible stories? If they are from God, we can't expect to fully understand them. We would do well to remember that what God gave the world through the Bible is not referred to as *explanation.* It is described as *revelation.* Explain the Trinity, the Virgin Birth, the Holy Spirit, the Cross, the Resurrection? I don't think so. And so, at Willimon's urging, we must attempt to "describe" rather than "explain" the mystery of mercy.

Untamed by common sense, mercy prompts reckless abandon. It urges us to reach out to others in ways that will benefit them but might make us appear foolish. On occasion, I'll drop by a laundromat and dispense quarters to whomever happens to be there. I haven't forgotten the days when I had to wash my clothes in a public laundromat. My sympathy goes out to those moms and dads who work all day and then have to spend their evenings at the laundromat. And so, I share God's mercy in an effort to say, "Somebody thinks you are important."

One of the most vivid descriptions of mercy is found in the parable of the man known as the Good Samaritan:

> A certain man was going down from Jerusalem to Jericho; and he fell among robbers, and they stripped him and beat him, and went off leaving him half dead. And by chance a certain priest was going down on that road, and when he saw him, he passed by on the other side. And likewise a Levite also, when he came to the place and saw him, passed by on the other side.
>
> But a certain Samaritan, who was on a journey, came upon him; and when he saw him, he felt compassion, and came to him, and bandaged up his wounds, pouring oil and wine on them; and he put him on his own beast, and brought him to an inn, and took care of him. And on the next day he took out two denarii and gave them to the innkeeper and

said, "Take care of him; and whatever more you spend, when I return, I will repay you." Which of these three do you think proved to be a neighbor to the man who fell into the robbers' hands? (Luke 10:30–36 NASB)

The response was simple: The one who showed mercy.

Mercy Takes Risks

But the kind neighbor in Jesus' story did all the "wrong things" according to society's standards of shrewdness. He didn't ask for the wounded man's identification. He didn't know the circumstances surrounding his condition. For all he knew, he might have been helping an irresponsible beggar. The Samaritan even left a blank check for the innkeeper. How did he know the injured stranger wouldn't run up an unnecessary food bill? How could he be sure the manager wouldn't gouge him with high restaurant prices? Just how did he know this wasn't all a scam? Come on, is this guy a good Samaritan or an airhead?

According to Jesus, he did the right thing.

One of the mysteries of mercy is that it coerces us to be sacrificially giving for the welfare of another—even a complete stranger—at the risk of being taken advantage of.

When we suit up as a volunteer, we are covered only by the cloak of vulnerability. Isn't this what God did? Wasn't there certain jeopardy in suiting up in the flesh? And when he allowed the slaughter of his own Son and many disciples, didn't he know that many would not respond to the salvation they died for?

Aren't we glad that God loved us so much that he was willing to pay that price? "For while we were still helpless, at the right time Christ died for the ungodly. . . . But God demonstrates His own love toward us, in that while we were yet sinners, Christ died for us" (Rom. 5:6, 8 NASB). This is a statement of mercy. We love what God did. And we want to be like him in our encounters with others. Even so, we are afraid. The words of Brennan Manning reflect many of us:

> We begin to resemble the leading character in Eugene O'Neill's play, *The Great God Brown:* "Why am I afraid to dance, I who love music and rhythm and grace and song and laughter? Why am I afraid to live, I who love life and the beauty of flesh and the living colors of the earth and sky and sea? Why am I afraid to love, I who love love?"2

And why are we afraid to care when we love caring? Why are we afraid to help others when we love to see people helped? Why are we afraid to risk when we are bored with routine's nonproductivity?

We may simply suffer from timidity. Peter encourages us to step out in faith: "God has not given us a spirit of timidity, but of power and love and discipline" (2 Tim. 1:7 NASB). It seems that God expects us to push the borders of the status quo in order to extend his mercy to hurting souls.

Mercy overrides safety and rationalization. It takes risks. And remember, God only risks it for us when we risk it for others.

Mercy Is a Window for Truth

Mercy's mystery grows as we see that it is often a window for the truth. In the story of the Good Samaritan, we found that only one man was able to see the truth of the wounded man's needs. The other two looked over his hurts and then looked away as if the casualty didn't exist. Their religion blinded them to the truth. They suffered from glaucoma of the heart! But the compassion of the Samaritan gave him vision to see the reality of the need.

Churches today could use a revival of mystery. Because we are focused on self-preservation—like the two religious men who passed by on the other side—we tend to avoid mystery and thus miss many truths. We like to be able to give answers that smack of intelligence. Rather than admitting that we don't know the answer to a perplexing question, we limit biblical discussions to the five or six areas we think we have mastered.

For example, a group of believers may be perplexed about the extent of God's working in the lives of individuals; they may worry that false teachings about mysterious miracles will invade their church. To avoid confusion, they confidently proclaim that God doesn't directly intervene in the lives of individuals at all! How dull! And how untrue!

Human nature fights moving into any terrain that leaves us vulnerable to the unknown. In avoiding the mysterious, many Christians—for fear of being vulnerable to untruths—have exchanged vulnerability for gullibility. They protect themselves by discussing only areas that fall within their comfort zone. Unfortunately, mercy usually doesn't fall within our comfort zone. We love to receive it, but taking the risks involved in giving it is quite another story.

The unknown is a key element in the kingdom concept. That's one reason Jesus taught in parables rather than scholarly argumentation. He emphasized the mysterious dealings of the heart rather than the power of reason. And after Jesus' ascension, the mysterious beginning of his kingdom on earth filled everyone with a sense of awe (Acts 2:43). Mys-

tery has been a part of God's dealings with people throughout history.

His dealings with us are so intriguing that we must
think like a child to get it! (Matt. 18:4). And why a child?
Children are fascinated by the mysterious. Jesus calls us to
recapture our child-nature and start over. Remember when
Nicodemus and Jesus had that famous conversation about
being born again? How did Jesus characterize true believers?
He said, "The wind blows where it wishes and you hear the
sound of it, but do not know where it comes from and
where it is going; so is everyone who is born of the spirit"
(John 3:8 NASB). That, my friend, is mystery. It's the picture
of a child who is born of the Spirit and does not know
where he is going or how it will work out, but he goes anyway.

Likewise, we are to pursue truth—wherever it leads
us—through the window of mercy.

Mercy Transforms

Mercy is also mysterious in its transforming power.
Mercy is radical and, therefore, perplexing. It doesn't con-
form to the image of the world. On the contrary, it looks,
thinks, and acts exactly like Jesus. Although our goal is to
imitate him in our everyday lives, we aren't always of his

inclination. Paul advised the Romans to be transformed: "Do not be conformed to this world, but be transformed by the renewing of your mind, that you may prove what the will of God is, that which is good and acceptable and perfect" (Rom. 12:2 NASB).

We need Jesus to help us with this transformation, and he does! If we were expected to do it alone, we might as well close this book and never look back. And we might as well clip out of our Bibles any accounts of mercy so they will hush their plea for greater compassion in our lives. Transformation is found in the mysterious activity of the Holy Spirit. We can't transform ourselves any more than the caterpillar can change itself into a butterfly. The Spirit is not a neat reference for Sunday-school talk. He is the Spirit of Jesus who chooses to reside within us. His presence in our hearts bears the fruit of transformation—and we are transformed into the image of the Jesus who roamed the Palestine terrain. And this fruit is not only for our own benefit but also for the benefit of others. "The fruit of the Spirit is love, joy, peace, patience, kindness, goodness, faithfulness, gentleness and self-control. Against such things there is no law" (Gal. 5:22–23). Much of this fruit is intended for outward distribution.

Charles Colson tells in one of his books about a special friend who offered to take his place in prison. While Colson was serving prison time for his Watergate dealings, a political colleague asked that he be allowed to take Colson's place and serve out the rest of his time. He knew that the Colson family was going through a grievous time, and he wanted his friend to be able to be with his wife and children and tend to their needs. The request was denied, but the example lives on.

How could a friend go that far for a guilty associate? How could a person willingly offer to take the punishment of another? Simple. As simple as the good Samaritan whose unintelligent act of kindness still can't be accounted for. Colson's friend extended mercy. And his mercy was active and selfless; it dared to risk everything for another.

the
mandate
of
MERCY

CHAPTER 3

So speak and so act, as those who are to be judged by the law of liberty. For judgment will be merciless to one who has shown no mercy; mercy triumphs over judgment.

—James 2:12–13 NASB

3

the
mandate
of
MERCY

Mercy has but one mandate: The level of mercy you show to others on this earth is the level of mercy God will show to you on Judgment Day. The way you handle those who trespass against you is how God will handle you. If you wish to receive mercy, you must spend it freely on others. If you set people free, you will be set free. If you will not let up, forgive, overlook, or drop it, then neither will he. He will make note of the regulations you lay out for others and will follow your lead.

Misguided Efforts to Improve Our Image

The mandate of mercy is often overlooked, though, because all our energy is focused on making ourselves look good on the outside. But this is a big mistake. When we focus on making ourselves look good, we invariably end up trying to make others look bad. If I have an argument with my spouse, it's because he or she is selfish and doesn't understand me. If my boss says my performance is not up to par, it's because my boss is unfair and demanding. If a brother or sister at church has an approach different from mine, that person's faith is suspect. And on and on it goes.

Our blindness to our own flaws puts our heads in a fog of self-deception and confusion. Our vision is blurred and the blame game escalates as we become unhappy and frustrated because others don't live up to our standards. We find ourselves in a continual state of agitation and frustration, and we wonder why our lives are in such a mess.

And because we cannot reconcile who we *should* be with who we *are,* we simply rearrange the rules for walking the walk, and thereby elevate ourselves. Michael Wells nailed our problem in his book *Sidetracked in the Wilderness:*

> We are commanded to live as depicted in Chapters 5, 6, and 7 of Matthew. As we try, we find we simply can't do it. Therefore, we develop a

Christianity that we can observe, one in which we can exalt ourselves and judge others who cannot arrive at our level. If we find intellectual pursuits easy, we make proper doctrine, principled church order, and discipline all-important. On the other hand, if we find intellectual pursuits unattractive, then our Christianity might revolve around emotional experiences, and those whose experiences do not match ours are held to be less spiritual.

In short, defeated believers are looking for the right thing—victory, a deeper life, something that will please God—but they are looking in all the wrong places."[1]

In order to shape the rules to our liking, we look down at the next guy with squint-eyed criticism. Hoping to find justification through our self-elevation, we find defeat instead. We rightly long for a life of righteousness, we seek assurances that we are prepared for the final day—but we look in all the wrong places.

I know the right place to look.

Mercy Triumphs over Judgment

If you want to be victorious on Judgment Day, the path to victory is not in viewing others with suspicion or in fault-finding. The hope of eternal victory is found along another path entirely—a path the world seldom travels. It's the path of *mercy.* Simply mercy.

The Bible spells it out for us: *"Mercy triumphs over judgment!"* (James 2:13, emphasis added). If it is true that mercy is the one thing that can bring us victory on Judgment Day—and I believe it is—then we must learn all we can about this crucial attribute. The story of Stephen in Acts 7 paints a picture of mercy that inspires us all:

> They cried out with a loud voice, and covered their ears, and they rushed upon him with one impulse. And when they had driven him out of the city, they began stoning him, and the witnesses laid aside their robes at the feet of a young man named Saul.
>
> And they went on stoning Stephen as he called upon the Lord and said, "Lord Jesus, receive my spirit!" And falling on his knees, he cried out with a loud voice, "Lord, do not hold this sin against them!" And having said this, he fell asleep. (vv. 57–60 NASB)

Mercy's mandate is that if we want to receive mercy on Judgment Day, we must dispense it here on earth. Forgiving others is not an option.

Write Your Own Script for Judgment Day

Let's look more closely at the passage in James 2, which we referred to earlier: "So speak and so act, as those who are to be judged by the law of liberty. For judgment will be merciless to one who has shown no mercy; mercy triumphs over judgment." (vv. 12–13 NASB).

Whether we go to the right or to the left on that great day will be determined by how we judge others here on earth. The "speak and act" of this verse is not referring to doing good or bad in general; it is specifically addressing how we treat others regarding our judgment of them. When casting the unforgiving servant into jail, the king in Jesus' parable rebuked the servant with these words: "Shouldn't you have had mercy on your fellow servant just as I had on you?" (Matt. 18:33).

If we choose to be merciful to others, then mercy is ours. If we demand an eye for an eye, that is how we will be treated on Judgment Day. "Because judgment without mercy will be shown to anyone who has not been merciful."

In other words, we each write our own script for Judgment Day. When the adulterous woman was brought before Jesus in John 8, all those who were given opportunity to cast the first stone walked away in unanimous admission of their own guilt. That story alone should motivate us to express great mercy in every direction.

The frightening but wonderful truth is that we all have a choice.

We Reap What We Sow

Jesus consistently stressed the relationship of mercy to our eternal salvation:

> I tell you the truth, whatever you bind on earth will be bound in heaven, and whatever you loose on earth will be loosed in heaven. (Matt. 18:18)

Perhaps part of what Jesus means in Matthew 18 is that whatever we bind in judging others on earth will be applied to us when we reach the other side.

> Forgive us our debts, as we also have forgiven our debtors. (Matt. 6:12)

Jesus seems to be saying, here, that how we receive forgiveness is determined by how we spend it.

> For if you forgive men when they sin against you, your heavenly Father will also forgive you. But if you do not forgive men their sins, your Father will not forgive your sins. (Matt. 6:14–15)

There is nothing left to say. He makes it perfectly clear that our forgiveness from him is dependent upon our forgiveness toward others.

> Do not judge, or you too will be judged. For in the same way you judge others, you will be judged, and with the measure you use, it will be measured to you. (Matt. 7:2)

It looks to me like he's got some sort of theme going on here!

> Why do you look at the speck of sawdust in your brother's eye and pay no attention to the plank in your own eye? . . . You hypocrite, first take the plank out of your own eye, and then you will see clearly to remove the speck from your brother's eye.(Matt. 7:3, 5)

Jesus uses fearless, clear wording here to get us to understand that whenever we get snippy about someone else's shortcomings, we are not seeing ourselves for who we really are. And what is it that we are bringing complaint about in the brother's eye? Note this: It is only a speck. (And we thought it was such a big deal.) It's not that our brother's offenses are to be diminished. It's that ours are understated as well as underrated. We have not a clue as to the disappointment our own sin brings to God's heart.

Jesus expresses in absolute terms that any time we are critical of others, we are blinded to our own shortcomings. For that, he reserves the most harsh terminology: "You hypocrite."

But Jesus also tells the other side of the story. When we are merciful and kind and forgiving, that is how God will treat us.

> Love your enemies, do good to them, and lend to them without expecting to get anything back. Then your reward will be great, and you will be sons of the Most High, because he is kind to the ungrateful and wicked. Be merciful, just as your Father is merciful.
>
> Do not judge, and you will not be judged. Do not condemn, and you will not be condemned. Forgive, and you will be forgiven. Give, and it will be given to you. A good measure, pressed down, shaken together and running over, will be poured into your lap. For with the measure you use, it will be measured to you. (Luke 6:35–38)

If only Wall Street were as faithful in giving returns for investment! Whatever we hand out, we get back. Sounds a lot like another heavenly wisdom you've probably heard: *"A man reaps what he sows"* (Gal. 6:7, emphasis added).

Now might be a good time to contemplate whether there is someone in your life you need to forgive. If you refuse to forgive individuals who have offended you, you can't expect God to forgive you. This truth is backed by the seriousness and strength of the Cross. Refusal to forgive others separates us from God.

Mercy in the Face of Persecution

The Bible makes it ultra-clear that Judgment Day is coming and that our faith sets the stage for how it will all wash out. The first-century Christians relied on the promise of heaven to give them strength in times of persecution. The Hebrew writer urges them to keep on practicing mercy.

> Remember those earlier days after you had received the light, when you stood your ground in a great contest in the face of suffering. Sometimes you were publicly exposed to insult and persecution; at other times you stood side by side with those who were so treated. You sympathized with those in prison and joyfully accepted the confiscation of your property, because you knew that you yourselves had better and lasting possessions.
>
> So do not throw away your confidence; it will

be richly rewarded. You need to persevere so that when you have done the will of God, you will receive what he has promised. (Heb. 10:32–36)

What was promised? Mercy to all who had shown it. Look at their actions. They suffered and became public spectacles yet remained sympathetic and happy. They gladly took it on the chin. Like the first-century Christians, we, too, can gain mercy by giving it to others. Not only is mercy God's message to us and expectation of us, it's his style on earth. The Cross is mercy made in heaven, and it shocks the world even now.

The Hebrew writer continues to encourage the Christians in the next few verses. "For in just a very little while, 'He who is coming will come and will not delay. But my righteous one will live by faith. And if he shrinks back, I will not be pleased with him.' But we are not of those who shrink back and are destroyed, but of those who believe and are saved" (Heb. 10:37–39).

Shrinking back? Who is he talking about? I think the context insists that it refers to those who will not endure harsh and unfair treatment by loving their enemies and faithfully trusting in the Lord to deliver the judgment.

Opportunities to shrink back from harsh treatment in fear or frustration are abundant—they may even lurk in your own home. But you *can* repay offense with mercy. As long as you continue to put your faith in God, you can show mercy even to the crustiest codger you know.

It should be no surprise that mercy plays a significant role in judgment. It has always been a vital part of God's heart and process. During the first covenant, written about in the Old Testament, the Holy of Holies section of the tabernacle was sacred because God's presence dwelt there. Golden cherubim overshadowed the mercy seat. Angels guarded God's dwelling place—the place of *mercy*. Notice that it wasn't called the seat of work, money, or miracles. Rather, at the center of the dwelling place of God was a seat called mercy. And the mandate of mercy for us is that on that Great Day we will receive what we dispensed here on earth.

the meaning of MERCY

CHAPTER 4

By grace you have been saved through faith; and that not of yourselves, it is a gift of God; not as a result of works, that no one should boast.

—Ephesians 2:8–9 NASB

4

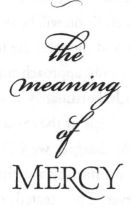

the
meaning
of
MERCY

Can you imagine having the assignment of describing the Pacific Ocean by examining a quart jar full of sea water? Or how about trying to gather comprehensive information about the Rocky Mountains with a camera and a roll of film? When astronauts gather research from outer space with their "technologically advanced" robot, what percentage of God's vast universe do they really reveal to us?

How much more overwhelming to attempt to explain the meaning of mercy—an essential spiritual element of God—in one chapter? Efforts to capture the completeness of any given particle of God are inadequate. After all, we have nothing more to work with than a quart jar, a camera, and a robot!

Thus we will approach our discussion on the meaning of mercy aware that our definition will be sketchy at best. When Isaiah said God's ways and thoughts are higher than ours, he told us the truth. Our only approach for insight is through the dim window of faith. Fortunately, that faith gives us both the conviction and the hope of the existence of mercy.

Learn, we will. Be charged, we will. Gain enthusiasm, we will. But close in on him by a definition? An explanation? A diagram? Never! The created will never snare the entire *anything* of the Creator. "Oh, the depth of the riches of the wisdom and knowledge of God! How unsearchable his judgments, and his paths beyond tracing out!" (Rom. 11:33). This truth insists that we be in awe of the indescribable dimensions of God. Yet for all God's "unsearchableness" and "unfathomableness," he openly invites us to examine him. And so we will try.

We begin by noting the more obvious characteristics of mercy and her first cousin grace. A standard, proverb-like definition of these relatives has been "Grace is getting something we don't deserve, and mercy is not getting something we do deserve." I would add this: Mercy, also, is not giving others something they deserve.

The Power of Grace to Provide

Grace is divine participation in human weakness, and it functions in two ways: (1) It provides the ability to accomplish things we cannot accomplish on our own, and (2) it provides salvation where there is no merit.

Grace Provides the Ability to Accomplish Impossible Tasks

Regarding its first function, Paul writes in 2 Corinthians 8:1: "We want you to know about the grace that God has given the Macedonian churches." What follows in that passage is a glowing narration of a powerless, even impoverished, church that accomplished the impossible by his grace. Later in the same book Paul says, "God is able to make all grace abound to you, so that in all things at all times, having all that you need, you will abound in every good work" (2 Cor. 9:8). The power grace gives to a powerless person is mightily emphasized when the Lord confounds the wisdom of the world by saying, "My grace is sufficient for you, for my power is made perfect in weakness." And Paul responds by saying, "Therefore I will boast all the more gladly about my weaknesses, so that Christ's power may rest on me" (2 Cor. 12:9). Grace turns our inability into powerful accomplishment!

Grace Provides Salvation for the Undeserving

The same apostle talks about the second function of grace—our eternal salvation—when he says, "For it is by grace you have been saved, through faith—and this not from yourselves, it is the gift of God—not by works, so that no one can boast" (Eph. 2:8–9).

Both functions of grace come in one format—a gift. Grace gives us a salvation that we are totally unable to attain on our own and that we absolutely don't deserve, and it gives us the power to accomplish what we cannot accomplish on our own.

The Power of Mercy in Relationships

Mercy is grace with a twist. Where grace applies to our lives regarding the ability to do things we can't do on our own (like endure hardship or grow spiritually or gain eternal salvation), mercy applies to our relationships with other people. It provides power for restoring and maintaining relationships—power that we don't possess on our own. Both mercy and grace are gifts from God. Grace applies his arm to the labor required of us when we are weak. Mercy applies his strength to relationships required of us when we can't make them work. Each enables us to do what we could not do on our own.

Mercy, like grace, is divine participation in human weakness. But mercy's emphasis is on *not* giving us the "justice" we deserve. Rather than cutting us off from his continued blessings—as we deserve—God gives us another chance . . . and another . . . and another. Mercy, however, is a double-edged sword, and with its blessings come responsibilities. Mercy calls upon us to bless others in ways they do not deserve—just as our heavenly Father blesses us, though we are undeserving. Mercy, like grace, also has two functions: (1) Mercy blesses those who offend us—even though we resolutely feel they do not deserve it and even if they don't ask for it, and (2) mercy blesses the "underdogs" and downtrodden of society—those who want to be in our presence but have no particular social pull to warrant our attention.

Mercy Enables Us to Forgive Undeserving Offenders

One monumental aspect of the first function of God's mercy toward us is his willingness to forgive our huge debt even though we don't have a clue as to the depth and seriousness of our offense. Therefore, the mandate of mercy, which we discussed in the previous chapter, is that we forgive others—even when they can't fathom the depth of hurt they've put upon us. It involves the feeling of compassion and the ability to release—to let things go.

God gives us a picture of the extensive forgiveness of mercy in one New Testament story.

> The kingdom of heaven is like a king who wanted to settle accounts with his servants. As he began the settlement, a man who owed him ten thousand talents was brought to him. Since he was not able to pay, the master ordered that he and his wife and his children and all that he had be sold to repay the debt.

> The servant fell on his knees before him. "Be patient with me," he begged, "and I will pay back everything." The servant's master took pity on him, canceled the debt and let him go.

> But when that servant went out, he found one of his fellow servants who owed him a hundred denarii. He grabbed him and began to choke him. "Pay back what you owe me!" he demanded.

> His fellow servant fell to his knees and begged him, "Be patient with me, and I will pay you back."

> But he refused. Instead, he went off and had the

man thrown into prison until he could pay the debt. When the other servants saw what had happened, they were greatly distressed and went and told their master everything that had happened.

Then the master called the servant in. "You wicked servant," he said, "I canceled all that debt of yours because you begged me to. Shouldn't you have had mercy on your fellow servant just as I had on you?" In anger his master turned him over to the jailers to be tortured, until he should pay back all he owed.

This is how my heavenly Father will treat each of you unless you forgive your brother from your heart. (Matt. 18:23–35)

The point? Remember how much God has forgiven you before you decide you can no longer endure injury from another. And contemplate the vast difference between the absolute purity and holiness of God and the sin and shame in your own life. In that light, the offense of another toward you is insignificant. In Jesus' parable, the first servant owed a *huge* debt and was freely forgiven; the second servant owed a very small debt in comparison, yet the forgiven servant showed him no mercy. The infractions committed against you by someone else are minor compared to those we commit against God. The mandate of mercy is violated when the forgiven sponge, full of promises, refuses to apply the Golden Rule to a peer.

Notice, also, that the first slave did not *ask* the supervisor to forgive his debt. He only asked for more time. Yet the generous master, of his own initiative, forgave the debt. That is a picture of God blessing beyond our requests. And this, too, God asks of us. We are to extend mercy not only to those who don't deserve it but also to those who don't even ask for it.

Mercy Calls Us to Love the Unlovable

The second function of mercy calls us to bring people whom the world scorns into our circle; it moves us to include them in the limitless love of God, along with the rest of us. This call requires us to leave our comfort zones and live in the shoes of others. It is the very quality of God that is desperately needed in his people today. As we extend mercy to our sad and lonely world, we infuse it with heavenly sympathy, empathy, compassion, and understanding. And these properties will shake the earth . . . for good and for eternity.

Some situations, however, seem outside the bounds of mercy. . . . You may be familiar with the heated debate that was aired on CNN on February 3, 1998, concerning Karla Faye Tucker's scheduled execution. Karla had been convicted and declared guilty of the brutal slaying of two people. Whether to execute her was a hotbed of debate. Nuns, pastors, and politicians stood on both sides of the argument and outrage.

Why the debate if she were truly guilty of these horrid murders? Because since her imprisonment, Karla Faye had been born again. Some doubted her conversion. Others defended her sincerity. The air was heavy with heated opinion. Following her execution, the words of Ron Carlson pierced my soul: "Karla Faye Tucker should never have been executed. She was born again. She was a new person." Ron's merciful statement might not seem all that unusual until you recall that Karla Faye had killed Ron Carlson's sister with a pickax.

The brutal crimes of Karla Faye Tucker are definitely outside our comfort zone for mercy. But Jesus' "Big Trip to Earth" was motivated by sins such as Karla Faye's . . . and yours . . . and mine. His love and compassion moved him to bring you and me and Karla Faye—totally undeserving, worthless outcasts—into his circle of love.

> Since the children have flesh and blood, he too shared in their humanity so that by his death he

might destroy him who holds the power of death—
that is, the devil—and free those who all their lives
were held in slavery by their fear of death. For surely
it is not angels he helps, but Abraham's descendants.
For this reason he had to be made like his brothers
in every way, in order that he might become a merciful and faithful high priest in service to God, and
that he might make atonement for the sins of the
people. Because he himself suffered when he was
tempted, he is able to help those who are being
tempted. (Heb. 2:14–18)

Jesus left heaven to bring us into his circle. Though we
are undeserving and undesirable, he loved us still. By expe-
riencing "earth-life," Jesus gained insight into our frailties
and thus was qualified to become our priest of mercy. We
are called upon by God to be priests of mercy to the misfits
and outcasts of our world. Recalling God's generosity
toward us prods us to be generous in like manner.

Being merciful does not mean that we excuse or overlook sin. On the contrary, mercy looks right into its face.
Then it compassionately pays the debt. We have one who
paid the debt from a cross. Why do you think he asks us to
take up our cross daily? There are sinners who need you to
give your life for them—who need you to be merciful

("mercy-full") in your dealings with them—that they can find aid in time of continued temptation.

Before we move ahead to the next chapter, consider Hebrews 4:16 and its use of both *grace* and *mercy,* and then rewrite the verse using our discussion of the meaning of mercy:

> Let us then approach the throne of grace with confidence, so that we may receive mercy and find grace to help us in our time of need.

Now, let's insert our definition:

> Let us then approach with confidence the throne of God's provision when we are bankrupt in any area, so that we may receive compassion when there is no way we can justify ourselves and may find his provision, which will be more than adequate to help when we are at the end of our self-sufficient rope.

When the meaning of mercy is lived out in our relationships with others, our *expectations* for them are matched by our *acceptance* of them. When a person falls, as we know people will, mercy keeps our acceptance from slipping with his or her fall. This mercy, then, instills the fallen one with courage and motivates him or her to get up and try again. That's the miracle of mercy.

the master of MERCY

CHAPTER 5

"To whom will you compare me? Or who is my equal?" says the Holy One.

—Isaiah 40:25

5

the master of MERCY

Brennan Manning aced it when he wrote,

> We get so preoccupied with ourselves, the words we
> speak, the plans and projects we conceive that we
> become immune to the glory of creation. We barely
> notice the cloud passing over the moon or the dew-
> drops clinging to the rose leaves. The ice on the
> pond comes and goes. The wild blackberries ripen
> and wither. The blackbird nests outside our bed-
> room window. We don't see her. We avoid the cold
> and the heat. We refrigerate ourselves in the sum-
> mer and entomb ourselves in plastic in winter. We
> rake up every leaf as fast as it falls. . . . We grow

complacent and lead practical lives. We miss the experience of awe, reverence, and wonder.[1]

God would deliver us from complacency and practical living if only we would let him. Wake up. Smell the coffee. There is wonder in our midst! And this wonder is not found in self-preservation. It's found when we live on the edge. It's found when we practice the miracle of mercy.

The miracle of mercy is available for all. We all have the potential to be wide-eyed and enthused. And we all have the option to be squint-eyed and critical—for we certainly have enough negatives in our lives to be sour about. Yet we can choose to find the diamond beneath the rubble.

Through Isaiah, God asked a potent question: " 'To whom will you compare me? Or who is my equal?' says the Holy One" (40:25). Referring to God's question, J. I. Packer writes:

> This question rebukes wrong thought about God. "Your thoughts are too human," said Luther to Erasmus. This is where most of us go astray. Our thoughts of God are not great enough; we fail to reckon with the reality of His limitless wisdom and power. Because we ourselves are limited and weak, we imagine that at some points God is too, and find it hard to believe that He is not. We think of God as

too much like what we are. Put this mistake right, says God; learn to acknowledge the full majesty of your incomparable God and Savior.[2]

Mercy is not man-sized; it's God-sized. Grasping the miracle of mercy begins with getting to know the Master of Mercy. It begins with acknowledging "the full majesty" of our "incomparable God and Savior." There is a difference, however, between *knowing* God and knowing *about* God.

Knowing *about* God versus *Knowing* God

Many Christians encounter a barricade to an experiential relationship with the Creator. It is called *academia*. We have wrongly thought that knowing *about* God is the same thing as *knowing* God. A brief look at two passages in the New Testament will teach us something of the blessings of knowing Christ.

Knowing That Surpasses Knowledge

In Ephesians 3, Paul asked God that the Christians living in Ephesus might know the love of Christ.

> I pray that you, being rooted and established in love, may have power, together with all the saints, to

grasp how wide and long and high and deep is the love of Christ, and to *know* this love that surpasses knowledge—that you may be filled to the measure of all the fullness of God. (vv. 3:17–19, emphasis added)

To know love that surpasses knowing? When we move from knowing (scholarship) to surpassing knowing (relationship), a whole new world opens. Paul says that knowing the love of Christ *surpasses* knowledge. We no longer know only facts; we now know the Person—the Master of Mercy.

I have met Nolan Ryan. But if you were to ask him how Terry Rush was doing, he would ask, *"Who?"* Although I know *about* Nolan Ryan, I do not have contact with him. I have also met Wayne and Marilue Huey. They are my good friends, and I stay in touch with them. I don't just know about them (information), I know them well (association). I *know* Nolan Ryan, but I have *surpassing* knowledge of Wayne and Marilue.

When a person has only met Jesus but does not relate to him, there is little to be amazed about. Such a surface acquaintance is usually nothing but burdensome. But the person who thinks about him, talks to him, does things for him, dreams about him, and needs him will find surprise after surprise in his presence.

The church is replete with facts about God. Yet a significant portion of her population feels disconnected. If this is true of the church, how can the unbelieving world know anything of our majestic God? Henri Nouwen hurt my feelings somewhat when he wrote with accuracy:

> Few ministers and priests think theologically. Most of them have been educated in a climate in which the behavioral sciences, such as psychology and sociology, so dominated the educational milieu that little true theology was being learned. Most Christians today raise psychological or sociological questions even though they frame them in spiritual terms. . . .
>
> Real theological thinking, which is thinking with the mind of Christ, is hard to find in the practice of the ministry. Without solid theological reflection, future leaders will be little more than pseudo-psychologists, pseudo-sociologists, pseudo-social workers.[3]

Real theology will include authentic relationship (surpassing knowledge) with God. Many spiritual leaders are guilty of knowing many things about Jesus but not relating to Jesus as real.

For some, he is more of a Santa figure than a real person

who identifies with our world. As long as we shore up our conviction that *we* are good, we will continue in the lie of self-sufficiency, believing that we need only a Santa-at-church to grant our desires.

But when we understand the implications of the Gospel and our complete need for God, our myths about self-sufficiency will dissipate, and we will beg for his participation. When this happens, a knowing that surpasses knowledge can truly begin.

Knowing the All-Sufficiency of Christ

Nouwen's statement concurs with Paul's insistence that Christ is all-sufficient. Instead of turning to psychology and sociology for answers to our questions, we, with Paul, must "determine to know nothing . . . except Jesus Christ, and him crucified" (1 Cor. 2:2 NASB).

In the following passage we see how Paul lays everything on the line in exchange for knowing Christ. He considers everything else *trash* when compared with the privilege of knowing Jesus. It is in Christ and Christ alone that we find sufficiency.

> Whatever was to my profit I now consider loss for the sake of Christ. What is more, I consider everything a loss compared to the surpassing greatness of

knowing Christ Jesus my Lord, for whose sake I have lost all things. I consider them rubbish, that I may gain Christ and be found in him, not having a righteousness of my own that comes from the law, but that which is through faith in Christ—the righteousness that comes from God and is by faith. I want to know Christ and the power of his resurrection and the fellowship of sharing in his sufferings, becoming like him in his death, and so, somehow, to attain to the resurrection from the dead. (Phil. 3:7–11)

Let us not dilute the power of Christ with our human philosophies and solutions. The Master of Mercy is worth knowing. But it must be on his terms, not ours.

God's Mercy Attests to His Majesty

Would anyone care to guess what characteristic God speaks of when he describes his superiority and his majestic and marvelous control?

Mercy.

Speaking to Moses, God said, "I will have *mercy* on whom I have *mercy*, and I will have *compassion* on whom I will have *compassion*" (Exod. 33:19, emphasis added).

Therefore, it does not depend on our desire or effort but on God's *mercy*.

The abundance of our lives does not depend on our *will* or on our *running;* it depends on God's mercy. One blessing of knowing God is that, in his mercy, he intercedes in our lives to bring about his good. A life full of mercy is a life full of God. A life without mercy and without God remains mired in the rut of the practical. All is dependent upon his mercy. Personal effort isn't the answer. God's blessing is.

Much effort is spent in the Bible persuading men and women that they are not able to go it alone. "For God has bound all men over to disobedience so that he may have mercy on them all. Oh, the depth of the riches of the wisdom and knowledge of God! How unsearchable his judgments, and his paths beyond tracing out!" (Rom. 11:32–33). Unsearchable! Unfathomable! Deep riches! All based on two coexisting conditions: our sin and his mercy.

Because we are disobedient, each of us has been imprisoned by sin with no hope of ever freeing ourselves. The pain in our lives is intended to lead us to his rescue; it proves our fallibility. Michael Wells is correct when he writes,

> The Lord spends considerable time teaching us to recognize the baggage and residue when it surfaces.

... The more baggage that one has, ... the more he will be aware of his need to abide. The more aware of his need to abide, the more he will open the door [of his heart to Christ], and, therefore, the more he will have Christ's life living through him. The person with well-adjusted flesh, with great natural talent, ability, and intellect, will most often not see his need for the Lord so dramatically and will be slower to open the door and manifest the power of the Lord, merely displaying his own fleshly capacity.[4]

Anytime people feel in control and somewhat confident that they have life on pretty straight, they need to think again. It is only by the power of the Master of Mercy that we are able to stand.

One of the greatest stories ever told illustrates this well. The ancient children of God were being heavily pursued by their enemies. Caught with armed troops behind and an unsurpassable sea ahead, they had nothing of usefulness to offer in this dilemma. "Moses answered the people, 'Do not be afraid. Stand firm and you will see the deliverance the Lord will bring you today. The Egyptians you see today you will never see again. The Lord will fight for you; you need only to be still'" (Exod. 14:13–14).

The people were caught. The Lord delivered. The

Master of Mercy intercedes. The children couldn't. The Lord did. The Master of Mercy moves. The people were told to stand and be silent. It isn't up to man who wills or to man who runs. It is up to God who has mercy.

> Then Moses stretched out his hand over the sea, and all that night the Lord drove the sea back with a strong east wind and turned it into dry land. The waters were divided, and the Israelites went through the sea on dry ground, with a wall of water on their right and on their left. (Exod. 14:21–22)

We will all gain the thrill of victory in our walks if we will let God run the show. He alone can make all things work through his breathtaking mercy. I urge you to step away from being practical and all of its restrictions of mediocrity. If it is to be, it is up to him. The power we possess is simply to believe in his power.

Only recently have I learned that God deeply desires that each of his children conclude one thing: *I can't.* As long as we give whatever we're doing "our best shot," the result will never be any more than our best. He cannot break into our stubborn pattern of self-effort. We must choose to stop the rhythmic behavior. When we conclude we are bankrupt of adequacy, the Master of Mercy can move.

I like what Erma Bombeck wrote in a column titled "If I Had My Life to Live Over Again":

> I would have invited friends over to dinner even if the carpet was stained and the sofa faded. I would have sat on the lawn with my children and not worried about grass stains. I would never have bought anything just because it was practical, wouldn't show soil or was guaranteed to last a lifetime. When my child kissed me impetuously, I would never have said, "Later. Now get washed up for dinner." There would have been more I love you's, more I'm sorry's, but mostly, given another shot at life, I would seize every minute, look at it and really see it, live it, and never give it back.[5]

Don't you love it? While we're trying to guide life on our narrow little track of *must dos* and *don't dares,* we forget that it is exploding with wonder all around us. The Master of Mercy will bring amazement to our lives—every day!

I've spent too many years focusing on the negative. Negative things said or done to me were exceeded only by the negative things I said or did to others. With a plate so full of negatives, I didn't have the wherewithal to sense anything like wonder or amazement. But I'm learning that joy and exuberance are not based on getting that "one big break" or winning Ed McMahon's sweepstakes. No, joy and wonder come from opening our hearts to God's kingly grace. "Wow!" is right in front of our noses. And the wonder of it all is that it usually does not come dressed in the robes of power, elegance, or wealth but in the rags of poverty, struggle, and a poor spirit.

Brennan Manning quotes a prayer of Joshua Abraham Heschel:

> Dear Lord, grant me the grace of wonder. Surprise me, amaze me, awe me in every crevice of your universe. Delight me to see how your Christ plays in ten thousand places, lovely in limbs, and lovely in eyes not his, to the Father through the features of men's faces. Each day enrapture me with your marvelous things without number. I do not ask to see the reason for it all; I ask only to share in the wonder of it all.[6]

May your predicaments prove to be his opportunity to amaze you. Fear not. Any place you are forced to surrender because you cannot fulfill the need is the very place that serves as the launching pad for God to show his stuff. If he can bring you this far in life, he can take you the rest of the way.

The Master of Mercy delights in you!

the menace of MERCY

CHAPTER 6

Y ou, therefore, have no excuse, you who pass judgment on someone else, for at whatever point you judge the other, you are condemning yourself, because you who pass judgment do the same things. . . . So when you, a mere man, pass judgment on them and yet do the same things, do you think you will escape God's judgment?

—Romans 2:1, 3

6

the
menace
of
MERCY

Philip Yancey makes an interesting observation when he writes: "People divide into two types: not the guilty and 'the righteous,' as many people think, but rather two different types of guilty people. There are guilty people who acknowledge their wrongs, and guilty ones who do not."[1] Mr. Yancey has struck an awful nerve. People are profoundly talented at being ruthlessly biased in favor of self. Nonetheless, we are individually guilty of much.

Echoing Yancey's comment is Rebecca Pippert. In her book *A Heart Like His,* she writes, "The good news is that while life is difficult and sin an ever-present reality, God offers hope and healing for all who need it. The bad news is that we 'all' need it! The only way we differ is that some of us realize our need and some do not."[2]

The Blame Game

We live in a time when it just works out better if the other guy is at fault. Jim Cymbala wrote these telling words in *Fresh Wind, Fresh Fire.*

> Just as our culture in general is taken up with a victim mentality, where everything is somebody else's fault, to be relieved by psychotherapy, government handouts, or litigation, so in the church people are saying, "It's the devil's fault. Don't blame me." No wonder there is little brokenness of spirit among us. Why pray and confess if your main problem is oppression (or possession) by an evil spirit that someone else needs to get off your back? Few Christians or sermons use the word "sin" anymore. Few sense the need to repent of their own wrongdoing. Rather, they look to the outside for a scapegoat.[3]

The "Awe-ful" Reality of Our Sinful Nature

Not only do we have the audacity to blame everyone but ourselves, but we take it a step further by bemoaning the sins of others, as if we could never stoop so low. Not the case, says well-known writer Oswald Chambers.

> Never disassociate yourself from anything any human being has ever done saying, "I don't know how anyone could do that. I could never do such a thing." That is the delusion of a moral lunatic. God will give you such a knowledge of yourself that you will know, in humility before Him, how the vilest crime could be committed. You won't say, "But I could never do that"; you could. Any human being is capable of doing what other human beings have done. When you see a criminal and feel instantly, "How horrible and vile that person is," it is a sure sign that the Lord is not in you. When He is in you, you feel not only the vileness of the crime, but say of yourself, "But for God, I am that, and much worse." This is no pious phrase to be dashed off glibly; it is the awe-ful reality of our sinful nature.[4]

We tend to perceive ourselves as better than the next guy. One way to evaluate your self-perception is to ask yourself if you ever thank God that you are not as sinful as another. Scripture tells of two men praying. One was quite proud of the good he had done and the dark deeds he had avoided, and the other freely and humbly confessed his sinful state. Scripture goes on to say that of the two men, the one who was sure of his goodness went home unjustified. For those unwilling to admit their own sinful nature, mercy becomes a menace—for the only way it can operate is for its recipient to admit personal guilt. As Chambers continues, "The Cross condemns men to salvation. We remain indifferent to the Cross until we realize by the conviction of the Spirit of God that there are certain things in us which are damnable."[5]

Confession—The Pathway to Mercy

In the middle of the twentieth century, Dr. Paul Tournier reminds us that there is only one way to rid ourselves of the spirit of judgment:

> No one can get rid of the spirit of judgment by an effort of will. As long as I am obsessed by a friend's fault which has shocked me and made me reproach him, no matter how much I say to myself: "I do not wish to judge him," I judge him nonetheless. But the spirit of judgment evaporates as soon as I become conscious of my own faults and speak freely of them to my friend, as he speaks to me of those which make him reproach himself.[6]

Mercy brings to the table two facts: (1) We are in need of being forgiven of much, and (2) the only way we can be forgiven much is if we realize we have sinned much. The menace of mercy is that it continues to insist on both particulars.

James 2:10 makes a hefty assertion when it says, "For whoever keeps the whole law and yet stumbles at just one point is guilty of breaking all of it." The point of this verse and its context is that if we trip up in one area, we are as guilty as if we had failed in all possible areas. It's one thing to confess that we all sin. It's quite another to confess that all of us are in the same sin pot. Do we think we can draw a line between our sin and theirs? Do we think we can distinguish between the *good sins* and the *bad sins,* the *good sinners* and the *bad sinners?* I think not.

Charles Colson, in his book *Who Speaks for God,* comments on an astounding piece by Mike Wallace on *60 Minutes.*

> Introducing a recent story about Nazi Adolf Eichmann, a principal architect of the Holocaust, Wallace posed a central question at the program's outset: "How is it possible . . . for a man to act as Eichmann acted? . . . Was he a monster? A madman? Or was he perhaps something even more terrifying; was he normal?"

Normal? The executioner of millions of Jews normal? Most self-respecting viewers would be outraged at the very thought.

The most startling answer to Wallace's shocking question came in an interview with Yehiel Dinur, a concentration camp survivor who testified against Eichmann at the Nuremburg trials. A film clip from Eichmann's 1961 trial showed Dinur walking into the courtroom, stopping short, seeing Eichmann for the first time since the Nazi had sent him to Auschwitz eighteen years earlier. Dinur began to sob uncontrollably, then fainted, collapsing in a heap on the floor as the presiding judicial officer pounded his gavel for order in the crowded courtroom.

Was Dinur overcome by hatred? Fear? Horrid memories? No; it was none of these. Rather, as Dinur explained to Wallace, all at once he realized Eichmann was not the godlike army officer who had sent so many to their deaths. This Eichmann was an ordinary man. "I was afraid about myself," said Dinur. " . . . I saw that I am capable to do this. I am . . . exactly like he." [7]

If society is going to improve and if the church is going to gain respect, we must be as quick to confess our own liability as we are to confess our neighbor's. We are blinded by huge planks in our eyes that reduce us to 20/400 vision. (Yet we are sure our vision is 20/20.) With blurred, erroneous, and dishonest vision, we feel confident that our judgment on the matter can be counted on as accurate. Hardly.

Give attention to a clear indictment on those of us who esteem ourselves too highly. "You, therefore, have no excuse, you who pass judgment on someone else, for at whatever point you judge the other, you are condemning yourself, because you who pass judgment do the same things" (Rom. 2:1). It is true. When we are critical of any, we admit our guilt of the same.

The writer of Romans continues two verses later:

> So when you, a mere man, pass judgment on them and yet do the same things, do you think you will escape God's judgment? Or do you show contempt for the riches of his kindness, tolerance and patience, not realizing that God's kindness leads you towards repentance? (Rom. 2:3–4)

These words make me do a double take. Just about the time I am ready to explode over someone else's faults, God reveals that he sees *mine*. I once believed that when my world wasn't going right, someone else was the culprit. It could have been someone in my past or someone in my present. It didn't matter which, really. But this passage from Romans forced me to leave such selfish denial. *I* am the one at fault. I didn't want to be. I had been sure I wasn't. But I was.

This reality doesn't deny that others injure us. It insists, though, that we are never without our own ignominious sins. I must share with you one more quote from Oswald Chambers.

> Most of us suspend judgment about ourselves; we find reasons for not accusing ourselves entirely. Consequently the definiteness and intensity of the Bible revelation prompts us to say it exaggerates, until we are smitten with the knowledge of what we are like in God's sight.
>
> If you can come to God without a sense of your own contemptability, it is questionable whether you have ever come. The most humiliating thing in self-examination is that the passion of indignation we indulge in regarding others is the measure of our self-detection.[8]

For many years, I did not possess a sense of my own contemptability. The truth of my state before God didn't have a chance to penetrate my fiercely defensive heart. I was so busy looking at the flaws of others that I never even thought about the possibility that I was lacking. As well as being stiff-necked, I was well guarded. Such a position is a lie. In addition to the Bible texts from James and Romans, I found even more.

The prophet Isaiah also contributed to the breakdown of my resistance. When Isaiah saw God, he instantly confessed guilt. " 'Woe to me!' I cried. 'I am ruined! For I am a man of unclean lips, and I live among a people of unclean lips, and my eyes have seen the King, the Lord Almighty.' " (Isa. 6:5). This great man of God had nothing impressive to offer—only his confession. In the presence of God, we finally see ourselves.

A New View of You

If you spend any time blaming your unhappiness on others, you need to know that it's not him or her or them. It is you. Real mercy can be a real menace if you live in denial of your personal deficit. When you can quit blaming a spouse, parent, sibling, colleague, or neighbor for your unhappiness, you will see mercy move swiftly and gracefully.

Some of you reading this book, however, may need no reminders that you are guilty. You know it all too well. Don't fight your conclusion. Realize that you are where we all need to be. You have reached your high point in life—if you direct the knowledge of your guilt toward seeking God. Don't allow guilt to burden and weigh you down; rather, take it to the throne room of God. Lay your guilt at his feet. He's been waiting for you to come. If he celebrated with the prodigal who returned from the pigpen, he will welcome you as well.

Philip Yancey, in *What's So Amazing about Grace?*, emphatically speaks to us all about our need to rely on Christ.

> The test of observance of Christ's teachings is our consciousness of our failure to attain an ideal perfection. The degree to which we draw near this perfection cannot be seen; all we can see is the extent of our deviation.
>
> A man who professes an external law is like someone standing in the light of a lantern fixed to a post. It is light all round him, but there is nowhere further for him to walk. A man who professes the teaching of Christ is like a man carrying a lantern before him on a long, or not so long, pole: the light is in front of him, always lighting up fresh ground and always encouraging him to walk further.
>
> In other words, the proof of spiritual maturity is not how "pure" you are but awareness of your impurity.[9]

Until our view of ourselves changes, mercy will always be a menace. It will insist that we be broken. I watch us take our turns in great pain, anguish, and woe. Some mature in this process of fire. Although they ache, they develop a peace, a patience, and a Presence that comes with brokenness. Others insist on fighting—they fight people, attorneys, courts, brokenness, and depression. To such people, mercy is a dirty five-letter word. Their *hearts* may have been broken by the pains of life, but it is their broken *spirits* that God is wanting.

Whether it be a global predicament or family feud, the daily news is filled with cries for mercy. The world is begging and pleading for a kind of people who can "have mercy on me, a sinner" (Luke 18:13). Not another ounce of hatred and bitterness will help. No more animosities are required. We have centuries' worth of suspicion and mistrust. The world's anguish will never go away unless . . . mercy has its way with each of us.

Let us begin to live on a higher plane—his plane, a higher level of loving, a higher plane of forgiving those who have pained us deeply. How do we find the motivation to do this? Is there anything more difficult? I think not. So this is how we approach our dilemma: We remember that we, too, have our moments of rudeness, offensiveness, misbehavior, and sin. We acknowledge that we, too, genuinely offend others.

It's difficult to see ourselves as complete jerks in any area of our lives. Yet surely we must consider this possibility since we cannot find one perfect person among the friends and relatives we have known over the decades. Surely we can deduce that we are not the exception to the rule.

The following words from the book of Romans remind us that we are sinners and attest to the miracle of God's mercy toward us: "God demonstrates his own love for us in this: While we were still sinners, Christ died for us. . . . For if, when we were God's enemies, we were reconciled to him through the death of his Son, how much more, having been reconciled, shall we be saved through his life!" (Rom. 5:8, 10).

If ever we struggle with being merciful as we happen upon an enemy, maybe we will do better if we can recall how it was when God happened upon us. When he found us, we were his enemies. Yet many of us refuse to take personal ownership of this biblical teaching. We can easily see how others are his enemy, but to see ourselves in that role is a different matter. Once we accept the true picture of ourselves, mercy will no longer be a menace. It will be a magnificent miracle.

the
miracle
of
MERCY

CHAPTER 7

Create in me a pure heart, O God, and renew a steadfast spirit within me. Do not cast me from your presence or take your Holy Spirit from me. Restore to me the joy of your salvation and grant me a willing spirit, to sustain me. Then I will teach transgressors your ways, and sinners will turn back to you.

—Psalm 51:10–13

7

the miracle of MERCY

All the king's horses and all the king's men never met Jesus. If they had, they'd have known one who could put Humpty Dumpty back together again. Mercy is the kind of miracle that puts broken lives and broken hearts back together again.

America needs the miracle of mercy. America needs mercy-practicing churches. Churches need mercy-practicing members. And members need to know that they are blessed by a mercy-practicing God.

But before we can learn to practice mercy toward others, we must learn what it means to accept God's mercy in our own lives. While God's offer of mercy is not dependent on our acceptance of it, in order for mercy's miraculous power to be unleashed in our lives, we must reach out and take what has been offered. Both God, the giver of mercy, and humans, the recipients, have a role to play in the unfolding miracle of mercy.

Our Role in the Miracle of Mercy

The story of the Prodigal Son is one of the most profound New Testament parables. What is it that makes it so extravagant and outlandish? The power of the story is mercy.

> There was a man who had two sons. The younger one said to his father, "Father, give me my share of the estate." So he divided his property between them.
>
> Not long after that, the younger son got together all he had, set off for a distant country and there squandered his wealth in wild living. After he had spent everything, there was a severe famine in that whole country, and he began to be in need. So he went and hired himself out to a citizen of that country, who sent him to his fields to feed pigs. He longed to fill his stomach with the pods that the pigs were eating, but no one gave him anything.

When he came to his senses, he said, "How many of my father's hired men have food to spare, and here I am starving to death!" (Luke 15:11–17)

Brokenness

This story paints the picture of a broken man. This young man went straight from prosperity to poverty. He was in such bad shape that he thought the pigs had it good. And that is quite a statement coming from a Jewish boy. Success had faded. So had his dreams. Nothing was working out. Even hope was dimmed.

This picture also portrays each one of us. Not every day, mind you, but we do take our turns at failure, bad judgment, and brokenness. Yet this is where the miracle of mercy begins. The only difference between the young man and us is that our pigpens are carpeted and have central heat and air.

When our lives fall apart, recovery is difficult. Sometimes it seems impossible. But the sequence of events that brought about restoration in this story is the same one that offers anyone and everyone complete and real optimism, and the first phase of that sequence is *brokenness*.

Acceptance of Blame

As we continue the parable, we see the second phase of

our role in the miracle of mercy—acceptance of blame. The life of our young character begins to make a turn: "I will set out and go back to my father and say to him: Father, I have sinned against heaven and against you. I am no longer worthy to be called your son; make me like one of your hired men" (vv. 18–19).

Accepting blame unlocks a life of blessing. Hear what he said: "*I* have sinned." Not *they.* Not *he.* Not *she. I.* The key to his upward turn is that he admitted his error. Unfortunately, many people continue to insist that whatever is wrong is someone else's fault.

His progress came, not because he faced trouble and overcame, but because he came to the point of brokenness. He admitted his personal failure and blamed no one but himself. "The move" that broke his fall was his honesty. He admitted that it wasn't his dad's fault and that it wasn't his older brother's fault. He blamed only himself.

God's Role in the Miracle of Mercy

As the story continues, we see that the boy went home to his father. Through this earthly father, we see our heavenly Father's role in the miracle of mercy. How did the boy's father react? He reacted just like our heavenly Father reacts when we come home to him.

Compassion

"But while he was still a long way off, his father saw him and was filled with compassion for him; he ran to his son, threw his arms around him and kissed him" (v. 20).

The phrase "filled with compassion" signifies "mercy." This picture of the father running to the bedraggled son is a picture of God running to you and me. Our simple admission of guilt puts God in a hurry to come to our aid.

We can hold on to misery by blaming others, or we can move into the arms of God's compassion by growing up and accepting responsibility for our sin.

Restored Relationships

Mercy is miraculous, for it restores relationships that are, for all practical purposes, dead.

> The son said to him, "Father, I have sinned against heaven and against you. I am no longer worthy to be called your son."
>
> But the father said to his servants, "Quick! Bring the best robe and put it on him. Put a ring on his finger and sandals on his feet. Bring the fattened calf and kill it. Let's have a feast and celebrate. For this son of mine was dead and is alive again; he was

lost and is found." So they began to celebrate. (vv. 21–24)

The father uttered not one word of rebuke. The father's gifts signal to the boy's heart that restoration is full: A robe is reserved for honored guests, a ring symbolizes a man of influence, and the sandals let him know he is not coming back as a barefoot slave.

Notice that the restoration occurred even though both parties were in very vulnerable states. The son could have feared that his father would reject his confession and repentance. The father could have feared that the son's confession was manipulative and insincere, born out of desperation. But each stepped out in faith, and the relationship was restored.

Mercy at work restores hopelessly lost relationships. "Was dead" and "was lost" are the father's words. "Is alive" and "is found" give reason for celebration. There is no way we can pay God back for the mercy and forgiveness he freely extends to us. No way. His forgiveness is only because of his mercy. It's a miracle.

Rapid, Unconditional Response

Notice that the father in this story told his servants to "quickly" bring out the gifts for his son. He did not put his son on probation; he gave him no trial period. He did not say, "I'll restore you as my son if . . ." Rather, he responded with forgiveness and mercy right there on the spot. A wait-and-see attitude may have been more prudent. Certainly, it would have protected the father's interests. But that is not the way of mercy. Mercy responds with lightning speed, without thought for its own protection.

The Miracle Reproduced in Human Relationships

God asks and expects us to reproduce this miracle in our relationships with others. It's not too much to ask. He gave first. He now calls upon us to play his role of *being compassionate, responding rapidly,* and *restoring relationships.*

Compassion

The Bible's call that we be compassionate and merciful to *undeserving* and *unworthy* souls is precisely why it is miraculous.

Recall that in an earlier chapter we considered the story of the Good Samaritan. The story says this man "took pity" on the wounded man (Luke 10:33). Jesus' admonition to us is that we "go and do likewise" by showing *mercy* to our neighbors (v. 37).

Jesus requires nothing of us that he has not done a thousandfold. We have only to remember the outpouring of Christ's compassion on Calvary to jump-start our own. Jesus died on roughly hewn timbers for our sins when he had no commitment from us as to whether we'd thank him or curse him. You gotta be kidding! Is this man from another planet?

Yes. And so should we be in the compassion we give to others.

Rapid, Unconditional Response

As we've seen in a previous chapter, Romans 5:8 says that "God demonstrates his own love for us in this: *While we were still sinners*, Christ died for us" (emphasis added). We tend to balk if the people to whom we are called to show mercy are "still sinners." We act as if forgiveness is too good for such scumbags. We want to wait until we can see the "fruit of repentance." Have we forgotten who died for whom? Have we forgotten what kind of scum we are? We want rapid, unconditional forgiveness from God, yet we turn to our neighbors in disgust and demand that they make total restitution before we forgive. This is not the way of mercy.

Because we each need to receive mercy repeatedly, our

forgiveness of others is to be seventy times seven (see Matt. 18:22). And the quicker the better.

Restored Relationships

People hurt each other. Friendships shatter. Marriages suffer strain. Coworkers compete for power. Christian brothers and sisters argue. Damaged relationships cry out for restoration.

Yet when someone causes us great pain, we regard it our noble duty to draw the line between us and them. And then there are those people who are so offensive that we just *can't* consider them "in the circle" or "in the loop." And so we draw more lines. But God calls us to erase the lines and restore the relationships. God had every reason to draw a line separating us from him. But he loved us instead. This is the miracle of mercy.

Attempting to restore damaged relationships involves risks and makes us vulnerable—as mercy always does. What if the other person won't allow the relationship to be restored? Even if restoration is not possible, mercy is. Mercy is not hamstrung by another's response. It is not dependent on the response of the second party. What if the other person spits in your face? If that happens, mercy just becomes more merciful by refusing to retaliate.

Of course there are some things that cannot be undone. Divorce often results in remarriage, so the original husband-wife relationship cannot be restored. And sometimes other circumstances prevent a broken marriage from being restored. But the love, respect, and kindness can be restored. The bitterness from my side of the fence can end—as soon as I want and as soon as I decide.

But, some object, people in their right minds would not expose themselves to potential rejection and abuse! Ah, but we are not in our right minds. We have been transformed through the mind of Christ.

We are required to show mercy in restoring relationships for one reason: God extended mercy to us in restoring a relationship severed by our sin.

Mercy opens the gates to restoration. Be encouraged. It's a miracle. My miracle to perform on others!

Making the Miracle Live in Your Life

Acknowledge Blame

King David did humankind a great favor by delivering us the fifty-first psalm. When David was confronted with his sin with Bathsheba, he blamed no one but himself. He drew God's attention to no other sinner. He asked only that God perform the miracle of mercy in his heart. His request was that his heart be cleansed.

> Have mercy on me, O God, according to your unfailing love; according to your great compassion blot out my transgressions. Wash away all my iniquity and cleanse me from my sin.
>
> For I know my transgressions, and my sin is always before me. Against you, you only, have I sinned and done what is evil in your sight, so that you are proved right when you speak and justified when you judge. Surely I was sinful at birth, sinful from the time my mother conceived me. Surely you desire truth in the inner parts; you teach me wisdom in the inmost place.
>
> Cleanse me with hyssop, and I will be clean; wash me, and I will be whiter than snow. Let me hear joy and gladness; let the bones you have crushed rejoice. Hide your face from my sins and blot out all my iniquity.
>
> Create in me a pure heart, O God, and renew a steadfast spirit within me. Do not cast me from your presence or take your Holy Spirit from me. Restore to me the joy of your salvation and grant

me a willing spirit, to sustain me. Then I will teach transgressors your ways, and sinners will turn back to you. (Ps. 51:1–13)

This man was guilty of raw sin. And he knew it. Crawling into a hole and dying was not considered. Blaming his past was not in his heart. Accusing his ninth-grade speech teacher was never hinted at. Unsure of himself, he was sure of God. Of all the others he could have mentioned, he mentioned only himself.

Human tendency is to place the blame on other factors: Wages are too low. Everyone else gets all the breaks. Taxes are too high. The teachers are too lenient. The teachers are too strict. The boss is partial. The employee is stupid. Athletes get paid too much. Judges are crooks. We whine and complain, blaming our poor performance on the other guy.

But the prodigal son and King David both direct us to a powerful key to making mercy live in our lives: When it comes to criticism, focus only on yourself.

Don't Compare Yourself to Others

When you finally admit your deficient and broken lifestyle, you may be tempted to be even more critical of others. When you see in others what was in yourself, you may conclude that they, too, are guilty of your guilt. After all, you've seen the error of your ways. Why can't they? When this happens, the accusing-blaming process starts again.

People have a mean problem of comparing themselves to others. That's often how we judge—we each perceive ourselves as the measuring stick. But we are not equipped to judge. God has said so. He has commanded us to avoid this pitfall.

Second Corinthians 10:12 is clear: "We do not dare to classify or compare ourselves with some who commend themselves. When they measure themselves by themselves and compare themselves with themselves, they are not wise." According to this passage, comparing ourselves with others means we are "not wise."

Read the rest of the story of the Prodigal Son. You'll find the second son sitting on the back porch pouting. Why? Because he was comparing his brother's disobedient lifestyle to his own obedience. He was comparing how his dad had rewarded him—the good son—with how he was rewarding this wayward brother. *Comparatively speaking,* he felt he had worked harder. The result? He was miserable, self-centered, and shortsighted.

When we abide by Christ's invitation to focus on him

rather than on our or others' performance, we will begin to experience God's mercy on a whole new level. Classification and comparison of ourselves with others is stupid. That's what "without understanding" means.

Choose Mercy

The only reason any of us has a relationship with God is because God *chose* to extend mercy toward us. Romans 9:25–26 makes a baffling comment: " 'I will call them "my people" who are not my people; and I will call her "my loved one" who is not my loved one,' and, 'It will happen that in the very place where it was said to them, "You are not my people," they will be called "sons of the living God." ' "

These people were nothing. Zeroes. But God *chose* to accept them. We, too, can choose to accept, love, and forgive those who have offended us and those we consider nobodies.

Just two verses earlier we get a glimpse of the thinking behind this miraculous inclusion. "He did this to make the riches of his glory known to the objects of his mercy, whom he prepared in advance for glory" (v. 23). He made a people who were nothing (you and me) into a people he called his own—simply because he decided to.

First Peter 2:9–10 reminds us of God's merciful decision to choose us, even though we had nothing of merit to offer.

> You are a chosen people, a royal priesthood, a holy nation, a people belonging to God, that you may declare the praises of him who called you out of darkness into his wonderful light. Once you were not a people, but now you are the people of God; once you had not received mercy, but now you have received mercy.

How can we not choose to extend mercy to others when God has been so merciful to us? The measure of mercy we extend to others will determine God's measure of mercy toward us (see Matt. 7:2). The choice is up to you.

The miracle of mercy is beautifully illustrated in the life of Corrie ten Boom, who was sent, along with the rest of her family, to Ravensbruck concentration camp during World War II for hiding Jews in her home. Rebecca Pippert, in her book *A Heart Like His*, relates ten Boom's powerful testimony.

> My name is Corrie ten Boom and I am a murderer. You see, when I was in prison camp I saw the same guard day in and day out. He was the one who mocked and sneered at us when we were stripped

and taken to the showers. We felt the shame of walking naked past this man. I could see my sister's frail form ahead of me, ribs sharp beneath the parchment of skin. He spat on us in contempt, and I hated him. I hated him with every fiber of my being. With every evil act he committed my hatred grew day by day. I knew that it was all right to hate evil. But I hated the sinner! Jesus says when you hate someone, you are guilty of murder. So I wanted you to know right from the start that you are listening to a murderer.

When we were freed, I left Germany vowing never to return. But I was invited back there to speak. I did not want to go but I felt the Lord nudging me. Very reluctantly I went. My first talk was on forgiveness. As I was speaking, I saw to my horror that same prison guard sitting in the audience. When he had last seen me, I was emaciated, sick, and my hair was shorn. I don't know if he recognized me at that point, but I could never forget his face, never. It was clear to me from the radiant look on his face while I spoke that he had been converted since I last saw him.

After I had finished speaking, he came up to me and said with a beaming smile, "Ah, sister Corrie, isn't it wonderful how God forgives? How good it is to know that, as you say, all our sins are at the bottom of the sea!" And he extended his hand for me to shake. It was the first time since my release that I had been face to face with one of my captors, and my blood seemed to freeze.

All I felt as I looked at him was hate. I said to the Lord silently, "There is nothing in me that could ever love that man. I hate him for what he did to me and to my family. But you tell us that we are supposed to love our enemies. That's impossible for me, but nothing is impossible for you. So if you expect me to love this man it's going to have to come from you, because all I feel is hate.

"You mentioned Ravensbruck in your talk. I was a guard there. But since that time, I have become a Christian. I know God has forgiven me for the cruel things I did there, but I would like to hear it from your lips as well. Fraulein—"again his hand came out—"will you forgive me?"

Forgiveness is an act of the will, and the will can function regardless of the temperature of the heart. "Jesus, help me!" I prayed silently, "I can lift my hand. I can do that much. You supply the feeling."

"Put out your hand, Corrie." It took all of the

years that I had quietly obeyed God in obscurity to do the hardest thing I have ever done in my life. I put out my hand. It was only after my simple act of obedience that I felt something like warm oil was being poured over me. And with it came the unmistakable message: "Well done, Corrie. That's how my children behave." And the hate in my heart was absorbed and gone. And so one murderer embraced another murderer, but in the love of Christ.[1]

There is no doubt about it—mercy is one miracle we can each allow to happen in our hearts. As our hearts bless those in our paths with compassion, restored relationships, and rapid acceptance, we concurrently receive swift and full eternal relationship with the King Eternal. What a miracle!

the *might* of

of

MERCY

CHAPTER 8

We have this treasure in jars of clay to show that this all-surpassing power is from God and not from us. We are hard pressed on every side, but not crushed; perplexed, but not in despair; persecuted, but not abandoned; struck down, but not destroyed. We always carry around in our body the death of Jesus, so that the life of Jesus may also be revealed in our body.

—2 Corinthians 4:7–10

8

the
might
of
MERCY

Lest you fear that mercy is out of reach—too difficult—let me assure you that inherent in mercy is the energy and strength to execute it. To risk again, to forgive again, to accept again sounds good in Sunday school. It looks good on paper. Yet where do we find the energy and stamina to repeatedly endure the rigors of this process? Never fear, mercy endows us with the power required for its expression.

Mercy Overcomes Disappointment in Others

Because others so frequently disappoint us, because we so regularly disappoint ourselves, because the weight of such failures threatens to incapacitate us, we need to be assured that mercy contains within itself the stamina to practice it. I love the way Eugene Peterson candidly describes his personal disappointment with others.

> Every time I move to a new community, I find a church close by and join it—committing myself to worship and work with that company of God's people. I've never been anything other than disappointed: every one turns out to be biblical, through and through: murmurers, complainers, the faithless, the inconstant, those plagued with doubt and riddled with sin, boring moralizers, glamorous secularizers.[1]

How are we to react when faced with such disappointment? How are we to relate when people fall so short of what they should be? In order to live rather than limp, we must latch on to divine power. How else could we love our neighbors as ourselves? Thank God, we are not required to do it on our own strength. We could not! We are always able where he gives us strength. Philippians 4:13 does not say that we can do all things. It says we can do all things *through Christ who strengthens us.*

God has planted within us a divine trait that enables us to give ourselves away when human nature would have thrown in the towel. Fear insists that we give up. Worry echoes the same. But these two bullies are nothing more than bandits who handcuff and then rob their victims. Only mercy can uncover the hope buried in the rubble of awful and repeated offense. Our frailty cries out that we've fished all night and caught nothing (see Luke 5:5). But a submissive heart is rewarded if we obey without understanding: "But because you say so, I will let down the nets." Like the disciples who were fatigued and sure there was nothing left, yet cast their nets in faith anyway, we too are amazed when Jesus comes through. He does strengthen, after all.

Mercy provides us with power to resist giving in and the strength to not give up. Preachers, therapists, and friends may weary. Their voices may remind you that you are exhausted and need to quit. Their advice may be that continuing will be the straw that broke the camel's back. But mercy knows no such straw. It has the might to proceed with more love, more kindness, more goodness. Is it not strange that these characteristics are the fruit, not of our efforts, but of the Holy Spirit? (see Gal. 5:22–23). In him we are enabled.

Imitating the Mercy of Jesus

In *The Blessings of Brokenness* by Charles Stanley, we read:

Goodness is expressed in forgiveness. When we are broken, we no longer demand of others the emotional debt they owe because they have mistreated us. We no longer attempt to manipulate people, control people, or punish people for what they have done or for what we suspect they might do. We don't hold grudges. We are quick to say in our prayer, "This person belongs to you, God. I release this person fully to you. I trust you to work in their life."

The goodness of God compels us to look for the good in others and to do whatever we can to build up others. Goodness prompts us to help those in need, to pray for those who don't know the Lord, and to seek justice on behalf of those who are oppressed.

Whatever Jesus did was good. When we experience the goodness of the Holy Spirit flowing in us, we will do the works that Jesus did, and we will be effective in doing them.[2]

Jesus' greatest work was to die for his enemies. As Jesus was being put to death on the cross, the Lamb of God uttered these amazing words: "Father, forgive them, for they do not know what they are doing" (Luke 23:34). Jesus possibly cried out to the Father from the cross until he was hoarse. Although shaken, injured, and fiercely wounded, he was still able to at least whisper at the end, "Father, give them heaven."

Brutal men were treating the Savior barbarically, with the full intention of taking his life, and yet he pleaded their case to God and said they didn't know what they were doing? He was either insane . . . or full of mercy. Nearly dead, the might of mercy instilled him with the energy to care.

I enjoy the sweet account Brennan Manning gives of his visit to an Amish farmhouse in Lancaster, Pennsylvania. Jonas Zook's family included forty-seven-year-old "little Elam"—who was about four feet tall, heavyset, thickly bearded, and retarded. Although Elam had never met Brennan, when Elam saw him get out of the car, Elam ran to him lickety-split, leaped into the air, and grabbed on to him. Elam kissed Brennan on the lips fiercely for thirty seconds. Once this new friendship had been established, Elam took his new companion on a tour of the farm.

Later during lunch, Brennan turned and inadvertently struck Elam in the ribs with his elbow. Brennan was totally undone when Elam began weeping like a two-year-old. When Elam detected Brennan's remorse, his reaction was spontaneous and from the heart.

Elam came over to my chair, planted himself on my lap, and kissed me even harder on the lips. Then he kissed my eyes, my nose, my forehead, and cheeks. In his simplicity, little Elam Zook was an icon of Jesus Christ. Why? Because his love for me did not stem from any attractiveness or lovability of mine. It was not conditioned by any response on my part. Elam loved me whether I was kind or unkind, pleasant or nasty. His love arose from a source outside of himself and myself.[3]

God deeply desires that his children imitate his Child. He wants us, even when we are exhausted and pained, to whisper forgiveness to those who slay our hearts, our minds, our strengths. Even as our fleshly energy disintegrates, the Spirit infuses us with the strength to stand up to those who hurt us—and bless them.

The Might of Mercy Resides in Death to Self

God designed us to be useful, merciful, fruitful for his glory, yet we are weak and unable. In 2 Corinthians 4, Paul explains that our human frailty does not prevent God from working his mighty purpose in us; rather, frailty is the vessel through which he best works: "We have this treasure in jars of clay to show that this all-surpassing power is from

God and not from us" (v. 7). Note the power. It is not *from* us, but is *in* us. As the text continues, we see that God's strength is intact in us, even when, physically, collapse seems more likely. "We are hard pressed on every side, but not crushed; perplexed, but not in despair; persecuted, but not abandoned; struck down, but not destroyed. We always carry around in our body the death of Jesus, so that the life of Jesus may also be revealed in our body" (vv. 8–10).

What a strange thought. Christians carry around the *death of Jesus* within them. We understand a little of the meaning when we remember how he died. He died forgiving the wretches. The same mighty mercy that flowed from his heart on the cross can flow from ours today. In fact, it is in the process of taking up our cross daily that we die to our selfish will while blessing the very ones who attack us. "For we who are alive are always being given over to death for Jesus' sake, so that his life may be revealed in our mortal body" (v. 11). This process is called mercy.

There is unique energy within the dying one to dispense love. "So then, death is at work in us, but life is at work in you" (v. 12). When we die to ourselves, we give life to others. Jesus did it. Did he die for the righteous or for the sinners? He died for sinners.

Stephen did it. As huge stones were crushing the life out of him, he screamed forgiveness over his persecutors. "While they were stoning him, Stephen prayed, 'Lord Jesus, receive my spirit.' Then he fell on his knees and cried out, 'Lord, do not hold this sin against them'" (Acts 7:59–60). That's what I call a great shouting match. Religious officials cursed Stephen; Stephen blessed them. If you are going to have yelling in your house, let it be in screaming forgiveness!

Use Your Energy to Be Merciful

Romans 12:14 requires that we use our energy to imitate Jesus and Stephen. "Bless those who persecute you; bless and do not curse." Then later, "Do not repay anyone evil for evil. Be careful to do what is right in the eyes of everybody" (v. 17). I know we are often battle weary. Why use energy we don't have to fight when he said we don't have to? Why not use the gift of power from above to do good here below?

The Spirit of Christ gives strength (see Phil. 4:13; 1 Tim. 1:12). We need it to be productive on his scale. Ours is too restricted. Andrew Murray writes in *Day by Day,*

> There are many Christians who know that they must not only believe in a crucified Christ, but in a living Christ, and they try to grasp it, but it does not bring them a blessing.

Why? Because they want to feel it, and not to believe it. They want to work for it, and with efforts get hold of it, instead of just quietly sinking down and believing: "Christ, the living Jesus, He will do everything for us."[4]

Strength Resides in Weakness

Denny Gunderson, in his book *Through the Dust,* quotes James S. Stewart regarding where true power resides. "It is always upon human weakness and humiliation, not human strength and confidence, that God chooses to build his kingdom; and that he can use us not merely in spite of our ordinariness and helplessness and disqualifying infirmities, but precisely because of them."[5]

Rebecca Pippert tells about her friend Doug. Doug was a fitness buff. He worked out diligently for years, until he suffered a serious injury. He then began working out at a rehab center. He was astounded at the difference in atmosphere between the two places. At the gym, people did not reach out in friendship. They were training for competition.

Death to Self Results in Compassion

In the rehabilitation clinic, Doug found that he was cheered on at every small step of improvement and success.

The gym allowed no room for failure or weakness. The rehab center celebrated even the smallest success.

Pippert says that churches need to be like rehab.

> God's compassion flows out of his steadfast refusal to give up on his wayward children. His kindness and tender mercies are abundant despite our unworthiness and defects. So if God, who is altogether perfect, is still loving and compassionate to sinners, why are we, who are sinful and in constant need of forgiveness, not merciful and compassionate as well?[6]

This question is sobering. If the Lamb has the drive to forgive from his cross, can we not do the same? What a curious thing to notice about Jesus. The last work he did from earth was to forgive those who despised, shamed, and tortured him.

The last great work remaining for humankind is identical. We are called to model Jesus' sacrifice day by day. Racial, social, parental, marital, and theological relationships are primed and ready for the might of the Cross.

God has called his troops to do battle in order to save a nation of lost souls. And people are wildly lost. The church is God's tool for reaching and reclaiming the hearts of all men and women. Indeed, his goal is being accomplished through his backward approach of extending mercy to our enemies. *So death works in us, but life in you.*

Mercy Comes Equipped with Batteries

When a battery-operated gadget is purchased, a label often says *batteries not included.* If the new owner has any hope of using her new appliance, she has to pick up the power portion of the package. Mercy includes the batteries. Power is supplied because the Manufacturer understands that we live with exhaustion and extreme fatigue.

The Hebrew writer gives us reason to stick to our plans in following the dying of Jesus effectively . . . with batteries.

> Since we have a great high priest who has gone through the heavens, Jesus the Son of God, let us hold firmly to the faith we profess. For we do not have a high priest who is unable to sympathize with our weaknesses, but we have one who has been tempted in every way, just as we are—yet was without sin. Let us then approach the throne of grace with confidence, so that we may receive mercy and find grace to help us in our time of need. (Heb. 4:14–16)

The theme? Don't give up just because you are about to give out.

If you are under threat from fatigue, give in . . . to mercy. Mercy is near and it comes packaged with power for you to do what God needs of you. He sympathizes with our weaknesses. He's not critical. Furthermore, he provides the stamina.

the measure of MERCY

Woe to you, teachers of the law and Pharisees, you hypocrites! You give a tenth of your spices—mint, dill and cummin. But you have neglected the more important matters of the law—justice, mercy and faithfulness. You should have practiced the latter, without neglecting the former. You blind guides! You strain out a gnat but swallow a camel.

—Matthew 23:23–24

9

the
measure
of
MERCY

God's mercy toward you is without limits, without boundaries, without restriction! . . . Except for one thing. There is one condition that can restrict the flow of God's mercy toward you. There is one person who can put a cap on the measure of God's mercy in your life. That person is you, and that measure is the degree of mercy you show to others.

"For if you forgive men when they sin against you, your heavenly Father will also forgive you. But if you do not forgive men their sins, your Father will not forgive your sins" (Matt. 6:14–15). In other words, the measure of mercy given to you on that Final Day will match the mercy you give to others on earth. If you allow people room for error, you will receive the same allowance. If you ruthlessly extend no room for transgression, you'll eventually find you have committed the fatal transgression. For the measure of mercy you extend to others will be measured out to you.

While God's mercy is mighty and marvelous and miraculous, it does have this one limit: "Use it or lose it." The only asterisk to ongoing, free-flowing mercy is that it will be withheld from us if we withhold it from others. Does this "condition of mercy" seem harsh to you? Personally, I used to feel that this concept was too harsh—even though my research seemed to point to it. But regardless of what you or I feel about it, the biblical teaching is clear. As we've seen before, the Bible is unequivocal in its proclamation: "Judgment will be merciless to one who has shown no mercy; mercy triumphs over judgment" (James 2:13 NASB), and "In the same way you judge others, you will be judged, and with the measure you use, it will be measured to you" (Matt. 7:2).

Why We Refuse to Extend Mercy

If it's true that the measure of mercy we give to others is the measure God will give to us, then we need to figure out why we have such a hard time extending mercy. Why are we are so stingy with the amounts of mercy we measure out to others? Why do we feel the need to shift blame from ourselves to others? Why are we so harsh in our judgments of others? The answers to these questions might open up whole new possibilities for growth.

Following are a few of the fundamental reasons we withhold mercy; many will find variations on these basic themes in their own lives.

1. We Believe God Requires Perfection

If somewhere in our hearts, we believe that God really does expect us to be perfect—in spite of all we've been taught about grace—then we are obliged to manufacture a facade of personal perfection, and we believe that our own efforts and worth will somehow gain us acceptance before God.

Michael Wells addresses our futile efforts to do it on our own.

> I coped with my defeats and failures in a variety of ways. I read self-help and how-to books which all promised to give me one-time relief. Those how-to books eloquently described my condition but sent me away powerless to escape. The more I read, the more frustrated, angry, and depressed I became. They told me of the great example of Jesus, how He

prayed, fasted, helped others, worshiped, was
devout, fed the hungry, and loved—and then they
told me to imitate Him! Didn't they realize that I
wanted to be like Jesus and I wanted to please God,
but I simply couldn't? Didn't they realize that if I
could imitate Jesus, He would not have had to
come?[1]

Self-help books and steps to success often leave the
seeker depressed and angry. Why? Because the prosperity
they promise is based either on the performance of self or
the performance of another in order to satisfy self.
Whichever, failure is inevitable.

A performance-based religion will kill our spirits. We
must come to the realization that we cannot help ourselves—and the sooner we realize this, the better. The old
adage "God helps those who help themselves" is overturned
by Paul's statement in Romans: "You see, at just the right
time, when we were still powerless, Christ died for the
ungodly" (5:6). *When* did God help us? When we could not
help ourselves.

And through Paul's admission of his weakness, we see
our own:

What I do is not the good I want to do; no, the
evil I do not want to do—this I keep on doing. Now

if I do what I do not want to do, it is no longer I who do it, but it is sin living in me that does it.

So I find this law at work: When I want to do good, evil is right there with me. For in my inner being I delight in God's law; but I see another law at work in the members of my body, waging war against the law of my mind and making me a prisoner of the law of sin at work within my members. (Rom. 7:19–23)

The verses that follow are most magnificent. "What a wretched man I am! Who will rescue me from this body of death?" (v. 24). Note the consistency with which Paul brings home this message: *I* am the sinner; not the other person, *me*. The Word is not shy in making certain we get this truth. Paul's answer to his question? "Thanks be to God—through Jesus Christ our Lord!" (v. 25).

Make no mistake, there are rules; but the rules have changed. We are no longer bound by the Law of the Old Covenant. Mercy changed the rules by eliminating the regulations. Getting right with God has been deregulated. Paul's response supports this. The answer to Paul's question lies not in a law, but in a Person. Jesus is the performer; we were unable to accomplish recovery on our own.

The kingdom of God is not a process of improving self;

it is a call to deny self and to seek God. This is why he said, "For whoever wants to save his life will lose it, but whoever loses his life for me will save it" (Luke 9:24). God does not call for improvement of lives based on certain steps. Rather, he calls for surrender of our lives that we might gain them back . . . now. Striving to improve our own lives will leave us ever wandering in a wilderness of futility. But surrendering all that we are will lead us to a marvelous possessed-at-the-moment eternity.

We like the idea of self-improvement because it offers steps that we can understand and define; there is little mystery to it. But all our efforts lead only to anger and deeper frustration, because failure is certain. The process of surrender is not easily measured because it is a spiritual process. "The man without the Spirit does not accept the things that come from the Spirit of God, for they are foolishness to him, and he cannot understand them, because they are spiritually discerned" (1 Cor. 2:14). Philip Yancey addresses the dulling effect of natural thinking.

> From nursery school onward we are taught how to succeed in the world of ungrace. The early bird gets the worm. No pain, no gain. There is no such thing as a free lunch. Demand your rights. Get what you pay for. I know these rules well because I live by

them. I work for what I earn; I like to win; I insist on my rights. I want people to get what they deserve—nothing more, nothing less.

Yet if I care to listen, I hear a loud whisper from the gospel that I did not get what I deserved. I deserved punishment and got forgiveness. I deserved wrath and got love. I deserved debtor's prison and got instead a clean credit history. I deserved stern lectures and crawl-on-your-knees repentance; I got a banquet—Babette's feast—spread for me.[2]

Remember our definition from an earlier chapter: Mercy is not getting what we deserve. It's also not giving others what they deserve. The miracle of mercy is based on the fact that we cannot do it on our own. That's why it's called mercy. Otherwise, it would be called something like earnings or dividends. Earnings are based on our performance. Mercy is based on God's. Mercy isn't of us. It's a gift from God to us, and it's a gift from us to others. Mercy is eternal.

2. We Can't Abide Being Wrong

This second reason builds on the first. If there is animosity between myself and someone else, I must judge the other person in order to make myself look good by comparison. My ex-spouse/neighbor/child/parent/friend/etc. *must* be the one to blame, because if he or she is not, then the finger points back at me—and I just can't abide that! Why, if I am guilty, then the facade I've built around myself will begin to crumble. If I'm guilty, then how will God accept me? How will I "earn" eternal salvation? But if I can somehow shift all the blame to the other person, I will be exonerated and thus maintain my "perfect" status before God.

But the fact is, I *am* wrong. I've done wrong, I've been wrong, I've wronged others, and I've wronged God. And that's not the worst of it: I can do nothing to make things right again. Romans 3 says, "There is no one righteous, not even one; there is no one who understands, no one who seeks God. All have turned away, they have together become worthless; there is no one who does good, not even one" (vv. 10–12). We're all in the same boat. We might as well admit it and look to the only one who can make things right: Jesus, our merciful Savior.

When we finally understand and acknowledge the truth that we are vile sinners without any hope of exonerating ourselves, we can begin to accept God's mercy in our own lives . . . and extend it to others.

Mercy isn't difficult. All it requires is honesty.

3. We Can't Abide Being Wronged

When another person wrongs us, we want justice! We want retribution! We want groveling apologies. If, instead, we open our hearts in mercy and compassion, people may never fully understand how much they've hurt us. They may never bow before us and humble themselves at our feet. We may never find equity.

But what's so intolerable about being wronged? In 1 Corinthians 6, Paul says allowing yourself to be wronged is a better choice than going to battle with your brothers and sisters. In this context, Paul chastises the Corinthian Christians for taking their disputes to public courts rather than handling them within the church family. He says, "Why not rather be wronged? Why not rather be cheated? Instead, you yourselves cheat and do wrong, and you do this to your brothers" (vv. 7–8). The same principle applies to us—whether we're talking about court battles or home-front fights.

Mercy looks into the error, sees the error, and then overlooks—not denies, but better . . . overlooks.

In the third chapter of Colossians, Paul said this regarding God's will that we extend mercy to others: "As God's chosen people, holy and dearly loved, clothe yourselves with compassion, kindness, humility, gentleness and patience.

Bear with each other and forgive whatever grievances you may have against one another. Forgive as the Lord forgave you" (vv. 12–13).

The text is loaded with mercy: "compassion, kindness, humility, gentleness and patience." It settles the real issue: We all have enough personal sin against God that our mouths should be shut. "Whoever has a complaint" is to be silenced when the Lord's forgiveness of our own sins is recalled. All should be sobered by the Bible's consistent and insistent call in the matter of mercy. Inventory need not go any further than self . . . ever! What does he say we should do? Only what Jesus did for us: When you are wronged, extend mercy without measure.

4. We Deny What We Can't Understand

Another reason we withhold mercy from others is that the boundlessness of mercy is beyond our comprehension. It cannot be sorted and filed. It can only be believed. That's why Fenelon wrote in the 1600s to "put aside your self-interest, and simply let God's will unfold around you. Everything He does for you is for your good. Worship Him without having to know and see everything."[3]

Anyone who deems it essential to know and see everything is, in reality, blind. The breathtaking, thrilling, invisible riches of God's mercy are concealed from the hardened heart. The blind are unmerciful until they get full explanation, full satisfaction, full restitution. "Woe to you, teachers of the law and Pharisees, you hypocrites! You give a tenth of your spices—mint, dill and cumin. But you have neglected the more important matters of the law—justice, mercy and faithfulness. You should have practiced the latter, without neglecting the former. You blind guides! You strain out a gnat but swallow a camel" (Matt. 23:23–24).

But we don't have to remain in our sightless state. Paul's prayer for the Ephesians is for us as well: "I pray also that the eyes of your heart may be enlightened in order that you may know the hope to which he has called you, the riches of his glorious inheritance in the saints, and his incomparably great power for us who believe" (Eph. 1:18–19). Enlightened eyes escort unlimited, unmeasured mercy into the heart. Those who leave the judging to God see excitement, enthusiasm, and happiness—even when wronged by another. Such people can see beyond the explainable. They are full of mercy.

Mercy's Limitation

If you have difficulty accepting the fact that mercy has a limit, consider the story Jesus tells in Luke 16. The drama is surpassed only by its message—and what a message it is! Because of its author, it is imperative that we believe the directive.

> There was a rich man who was dressed in purple and fine linen and lived in luxury every day. At his gate was laid a beggar named Lazarus, covered with sores and longing to eat what fell from the rich man's table. Even the dogs came and licked his sores. The time came when the beggar died and the angels carried him to Abraham's side. The rich man also died and was buried. In hell, where he was in torment, he looked up and saw Abraham far away, with Lazarus by his side. So he called to him, "Father Abraham, have pity on me and send Lazarus to dip the tip of his finger in water and cool my tongue, because I am in agony in this fire."
>
> But Abraham replied, "Son, remember that in your lifetime you received your good things, while Lazarus received bad things, but now he is comforted here and you are in agony." (vv. 19–25)

The "pity" requested by the rich man is another word for "mercy." But his request is bluntly denied. Why? Because in his lifetime, he refused to be merciful toward Lazarus.

Your life is the court where the game is played. Your behavior toward others is monitored by the Referee, and there is one rule to the game, one measurement of restriction: Help others or be denied help when the game is over. Mercy will be shut off from us if we shut it off from others.

This is a hard teaching, but we must not water down its potency. William Willimon warned of preachers like me who try to sugarcoat strong biblical messages.

> We preachers, often in the interest of misguided evangelism, are forever guilty of attempting inappropriately to bridge the gap, to domesticate the gospel, to housebreak God, producing a gospel that is honey to make the world's solutions go down easier, rather than salt or light. In fact, evangelistic preaching is deemed to be that preaching which renders the gospel "user friendly," the reduction of the gospel to a slogan for a bumper sticker, a church billboard.[4]

God's teachings on mercy will not fit on a bumper sticker, and they do not go down easy. Remember the servant of Matthew 18 who was forgiven the enormous debt, only to begin choking a fellow servant for the $1.25 he owed? God says that this man hit the only restrictive measurement of mercy.

> The master called the servant in. "You wicked servant," he said, "I canceled all that debt of yours because you begged me to. Shouldn't you have had mercy on your fellow servant just as I had on you?" In anger his master turned him over to the jailers to be tortured, until he should pay back all he owed.
>
> This is how my heavenly Father will treat each of you unless you forgive your brother from your heart. (vv. 32–35)

To say that the Lord puts up with a lot from us is a tip-of-the-iceberg statement. We can fathom neither the depth of our violations nor the grace that out duels our sin. One thing is clear in this passage: The Lord becomes angry when we highlight the wrongs in others while refusing to admit the wrongs in ourselves. This is the ultimate and unacceptable blindness.

In his book *Believe in Miracles, but Trust in Jesus,* Adrian Rogers points out the disaster of those who are blind yet believe they see quite well. "Those who like the Pharisees claimed they had no blindness, Jesus sent away blind. Those who claimed to be full, Jesus sent away empty. Those who claimed to be righteous, He sent away unforgiven."[5] When we are blind to our own faults but see clearly the faults of others, we reach the only limitation of mercy.

Aside from its one restriction, mercy is boundless, without measure. Its unending bounty brings awareness that we are involved in something truly eternal. Mercy doesn't quit. It doesn't give up on people.

As the meaning of mercy dawns on your heart, you will know a new freedom, a surprising joy. You will know of mercy without measure as you become an instrument in God's hand, dispensing his immeasurable mercy through you to others.

the
methods
of
MERCY

CHAPTER 10

F or you know the grace of our Lord Jesus
Christ, that though he was rich, yet for your
sakes he became poor, so that you through
his poverty might become rich.

—2 Corinthians 8:9

10

the methods of MERCY

The methods of mercy are totally foreign to the methods of the world. The world calls for aggression, retaliation, equality, and self-protection. Mercy's methods involve brokenness, refusal to retaliate, inequity—even suffering.

Mercy Is Preceded by Brokenness

The methods of mercy have their way in our hearts when we surrender to God and admit our need. Brokenness positions us to be merciful—even to those who are arrogant, greedy, and deceptive. When we have been broken, we are ready to be used by God.

For several centuries, down through many dynasties, a village was known for its exquisite and fragile porcelain. Especially striking were its urns: High as tables, wide as chairs, they were admired around the globe for their strong form and delicate beauty. Legend has it that when each urn was finished, there was one final step. The artist broke it—and then put it back together with gold filigree. An ordinary urn was then transformed into a priceless work of art. What seemed finished wasn't . . . until it was broken.[1]

Believers are never complete until they are broken. When brokenness is experienced—and acknowledged—the filigree of mercy remakes broken vessels into stronger, new, and even more beautiful forms. Imperfection is no reason to live in shame; rather, it is the pathway to mercy. We need not hide our brokenness in humiliation; instead, we are called to share the hope of restoration with other dismantled souls that they may see the handiwork of God, as he brings usefulness and beauty into their ruined lives.

Becoming "broken" is not an act of our will; it is something that happens to us. And although it invariably involves pain and suffering, it is for our benefit. It is in the unraveling of ourselves that we find ultimate joy and purpose, meaning and fruitfulness. To be broken is not a curse, but a blessing. It will feel wrong, but we must trust that it is part of the process of making us more beautiful and more useful for God's purposes.

Jesus' first public statement, as recorded by Matthew, brings hope to broken hearts. Jesus said, "Blessed are the poor in spirit, for theirs is the kingdom of heaven" (Matt. 5:3). This statement has not only endured the test of time, but it has also outlived contrary philosophies for successful living. Weak fragments glued back together form a vessel most useful to the Potter.

God says that his "power is made perfect in weakness" (2 Cor. 12:9). Weakness is a crucial element in the grand and glorious scheme of kingdom procedure, but the flesh struggles to avoid it. Fenelon makes a convincing argument in favor of brokenness:

> You ask for a cure to get well. You do not need to be cured but killed. Do not look for a remedy; let death come. Be careful, however, that you do not courageously decide to let yourself find no remedy. This can be a remedy in disguise, and even this can give aid and comfort to the self-life. Seek no comfort for self-love, and do not hide your disease. Let every-thing be simply seen, and then allow yourself to die.
>
> This death is not to be accomplished by any of

your own strength. Weakness is the only thing you should possess. All strength is out of place. It only makes the agony longer and harder. If you die from exhaustion, you will die more quickly and less violently.[2]

Indeed, we are tempted to try to iron òut the wrinkles and remove the stains in our lives by our own hands (see Eph. 5:26–27). But the wrinkles are set and the stains are deep. Eventually, we discover that the task is too much. We must be sent to the Cleaner. He, alone, is able to purify and cleanse us. It is only when we acknowledge our need that he is able to make us whole.

You may recall that the prophet Isaiah saw the throne of God and was instantly aware of his own intense unworthiness. He was heartsick. All he could muster was acknowledgment of his bankruptcy. Upon that confession, God's angels touched his lips (see Isa. 6:5–7), and immediately—not after weeks and months of evaluation to make sure Isaiah was sincere, but immediately—the Lord commissioned him with the awesome responsibility of speaking to his people.

God has his methods for extending mercy to his creation. His methods are not rooted in our performance or ability. No. His methods spring out of our brokenness. He takes chipped, cracked, broken men and women and lovingly recreates them, binding them together with the golden adhesion of mercy.

Those of us in leadership positions in God's church are often slow to submit to the process of being broken. How very much *I* needed to be broken. I was arrogant, self-assured, and vain—sure of my own ability. I learned that, in reality, I am nothing unless he makes it of me.

Whether leading from the pulpit, a counseling center, a recovery group, or as a parent, leaders are only effective when they finally fall to their knees, ashamed and pained over their behavior. Leaders are never the answer or the solution to another person's problems. They simply model "I am nothing, and he is all." If it is to be, it is up to him.

Mercy Refuses to Retaliate

When Joseph was a young boy, his older brothers sold him into slavery. Because God had been working in his life all along, Joseph eventually found himself in a leadership position within the Egyptian hierarchy, in charge of dispensing food during seven years of famine. During that famine, the very brothers who had sold him down the river stood before him asking for assistance. Joseph recognized them, but they did not know who he was.

> Joseph said to his brothers, "I am Joseph! Is my father still living?" But his brothers were not able to answer him, because they were terrified at his presence.
>
> Then Joseph said to his brothers, "Come close to me." When they had done so, he said, "I am your brother Joseph, the one you sold into Egypt! And now, do not be distressed and do not be angry with yourselves for selling me here, because it was to save lives that God sent me ahead of you." (Gen. 45:3–5)

Amazing. Simply, wonderfully, refreshingly amazing. Joseph had been severely mistreated by his brothers, yet when he had the opportunity to retaliate, he offered mercy instead.

To suffer injury without retaliation is a method of mercy. In fact, it's a miracle! The apostle Paul says that love "always protects, always trusts, always hopes, always perseveres" (1 Cor. 13:7). Many proclaim to be New Testament Christians. Their behavior, however, suggests that they are Christians only in theory and that the "eye for an eye" philosophy is what they live by when injured.

People are in desperate need of mercy. Everything from increased lack of respect to road rage evidences the need for the methods of mercy. Our world will either find mercy or it will find catastrophe. We will learn to bury the hatchet, or we will bury each other in hatred.

Listen to the apostle Peter as he calls for an other-worldly slant on our response to any who treat us unfairly.

> Slaves, submit yourselves to your masters with all respect, not only to those who are good and considerate, but also to those who are harsh. For it is commendable if a man bears up under the pain of unjust suffering because he is conscious of God. But how is it to your credit if you receive a beating for doing wrong and endure it? But if you suffer for doing good and you endure it, this is commendable before God. (1 Pet. 2:18–20)

God's mercy is so radical that Michael Wells says that it is "not found on our planet; it comes only from heaven."[3] Yet Joseph responded in the way that Peter calls us to respond. Joseph was a human, just like you and me. If he could live up to heaven's call, so can we.

Mercy Keeps No Record of Wrong

Philip Yancey writes, "Grace is not about finishing last or first; it is about not counting."[4]

Jim McGuiggan writes in *Jesus, Hero of Thy Soul:*

> The lady on the phone was really chewing on me:
> "That's the second time you've done that!" she said.
> The sad truth is, she was right. But it did enter my
> mind, as she proceeded to take my flesh off strip by
> strip, that two wasn't the magic number. I didn't say
> anything, of course, because that would have made
> it appear that I wasn't particularly concerned that I
> had done wrong. And I *was* grieved that I had done
> it. The facts were correct, but her spirit was wrong.
> The poor lady had been keeping a record of my
> wrongs. Love doesn't do that![5]

Mercy is not an accountant. Whether encountering a
crippled person at a gate or an antagonist jabbing him while
on the cross, Jesus did not consider their wrongs when considering how to respond. He consistently responded with
love. Was it easy for Jesus to respond this way? Did he
breeze through forgiveness? No. Mercy is for the devoted.
Its nature is rugged. Its character will not take the easy way
out. Mercy is rooted in a matchless love that is not of this
earth.

Mercy Doesn't Demand Its Fair Share

Jesus reversed the rules of climbing to the top. He climbed to the bottom and asked us to follow. Paul said of Jesus: "Though he was rich, yet for your sakes he became poor, so that you through his poverty might become rich" (2 Cor. 8:9). The methods of mercy are contrary to the methods of the world: Die to self. Be merciful to sinners. Take a beating. Spill your blood. Turn the other cheek. Be benevolent without cause.

Although the unbelieving world thinks the methods of mercy are crazy, it bothers me that much of the church thinks they are as well. We have strayed far from the uncomfortable life of surrender and moved into one that demands we all get equal pay, equal rights, equal everything. Great emphasis is placed on *getting my fair share.*

Jesus didn't call us to a life that is fair. But he did call us to an *abundant* life. In John 10, he said, "I have come that they may have life, and have it to the full" (v. 10). And isn't that what people are searching for—an abundant life, personal fulfillment, living life to the full? A life filled with mercy offers all this and more, but God's methods are different from the world's. The abundant life God offers results from caring about the other guy—even more than we care about ourselves.

The methods of mercy call for us to say "I'm sorry" more than "There, you've done it again," and "It was my fault" instead of "You can't seem to do anything right." Self-examination may be our best boost to the abundant life.

Mercy Results in Suffering

When my children were young and one of them would lose a game, I tried to point out that a kid on the other team may have been in deep need of victory on that particular day. If my child didn't make the cut, whether in sports or academics, I wanted him or her to be aware that the ones who did may have been in real need.

Although it was indeed very difficult, I tried not to interfere when my kids were treated unfairly. I knew they needed to be trained by it. I knew it to be a way of Jesus. I am afraid many parents rob their children of the privilege of suffering. We want to make everything all right—immediately. We feel that good parents should protect their children from all harm. I disagree. If we do, our children will grow up to be discouraged employees, frayed spouses, disgruntled church members, and impatient citizens because they assume there will be no lingering difficulty or distress.

We forget that we are called not only to believe in Jesus,

but to suffer as well. "It has been granted to you on behalf of Christ not only to believe on him, but also to suffer for him, since you are going through the same struggle you saw I had, and now hear that I still have" (Phil. 1:29–30). We forget that the call to "bloom where we are planted" requires that the bulb first die.

E. Stanley Jones, in his book *The Divine Yes,* tells an incredible story of a Christian who chose to suffer with Christ.

> Some of the outcasts of southern India became Christians. Some of the higher caste Hindus wanted to punish them and burned the fields of one of these Christians. As he went out to put out the blaze, they caught him and cut off his hands. This Christian had been taught by the YMCA secretary. However, the YMCA secretary was deeply incensed at what had happened and wanted to prosecute the culprits. He said: "Let's take up a collection for prosecuting the people who did it. We have their names." They took up a collection and sent it to this Christian, now handless.
>
> The handless Christian said to the YMCA secretary, "Sahib, you taught me the Christian Gospel and the Christian Gospel teaches us to love our ene-

mies and to pray for those who despitefully use you and persecute you. Now you are telling me something else. You are telling me to prosecute. How can I? You introduced me to Christ, and he teaches me to forgive. I am sorry, I can't take the money." The handless Christian took the hand of Jesus and walked into the future with his head up and his heart up in victory. I can never forget him.[6]

This is a method of mercy. Not a popular one, but a method of God nonetheless. Many view the church as a place to hide from suffering. Yet the Bible pictures the church as a group of people who die. Paul said, "We face death all day long" (Rom. 8:36). The methods of mercy sometimes lead to difficulty. But the Resurrection power of Christ consistently comes to the aid of the daily-dying kind of followers.

Mercy's Top-Ten List

God is serious about the methods of mercy. He has made it clear that we will be shown mercy only if we show it to others. This has forced me to reevaluate how I view my enemies—and I have a few, you know. Research for this book has exposed me as selfish, defensive, and more selfish.

The methods of mercy are right. They are the very heart of God. He lives and illustrates these methods on every page of the Bible. Because I want to develop these methods in my life, I have complied a list of my top ten enemies. This list contains people who dislike me for reasons I can't control and some who dislike me because I failed them. I pray for each person on this list regularly.

I don't ask God to give them what they deserve. I don't ask him to punish them for not accommodating and loving likable, personable, squeaky-clean me. That would be the selfish, defensive me offering such a prayer.

Rather, I pray that they be richly blessed. I ask God to bless their work, their walk, their way. I ask him to guard them, to provide for them, to love them, and to be merciful to them. I ask him to forgive them for their wrongs. I pray that the loveliness of Jesus fall into their lives as a great blessing from heaven. I ask that their interests be guarded and their paths be enlightened.

I haven't done this very long. But already I'm noticing that when I run into these individuals, something is different. The harshness is diminishing and kindness is blooming. Not with all, mind you, but I am able to detect a significant difference with many.

Jesus chose the methods of mercy when he came to save

the world. He chose to live by them . . . and die by them. As a result, we are no longer his enemies. Hmmmm. Maybe he's on to something.

the misgivings of MERCY

CHAPTER 11

It is not the healthy who need a doctor, but the sick. But go and learn what this means: "I desire mercy, not sacrifice." For I have not come to call the righteous, but sinners.

—Matthew 9:12–13

11

The misgivings of MERCY

Can this mercy stuff really be right? Doesn't it just let guilty people off the hook? That's exactly what it does. It declares guilty people innocent for no justifiable reason—except one! Jesus fell in love with guilty people and gave his life for their guilt. The sentence in the book of Romans that says we have all fallen short of the glory of God is the same sentence that says that we have been "justified freely by his grace through the redemption that came by Christ Jesus" (Rom. 3:24).

I find it ironic that so many people, especially devoted Christians, debate mercy. In an article titled "When Forgiveness Is a Sin," published in the *Wall Street Journal,*

15 Dec. 1997, Dennis Prager challenged Heath High School in West Paducah, Kentucky, for hanging up a sign that read, "We forgive you, Mike!" Michael Carneal, the forgiven one, had shot three teenage girls from that school.

Prager went on to challenge Reverend John Miller for urging his church at Martha's Vineyard to forgive Timothy McVeigh: "Though I am a Jew, I believe that a vibrant Christianity is essential if America's moral decline is to be reversed. And despite theological differences, Christianity and Judaism have served as the bedrock of American civilization. And I am appalled and frightened by this feel-good doctrine of automatic forgiveness." Prager had some misgivings about the dispensement of mercy. It saddens me when I react exactly as Dennis Prager did. How could he believe that Christianity is the only way to reverse moral decline while berating these teens for demonstrating kindness, gentleness, and mercy? I think these teens took a step toward reversing the decline and Prager missed it! While other teens are involved in date rape, robbing convenience stores, and "feeling good" with heroine, these teens took a stand and likely took a lot of heat from sources other than journalists. How could Prager call this a "feel-good doctrine"? These teens proclaimed a message of hope for a criminal whose life was in ruins.

I applaud these teens for demonstrating their convictions with a poster of mercy, in spite of the fact that their classmates had been shot. Many other injured teens choose to demonstrate their heartbreak by participating in theft, drugs, and violence. Thank you, West Paducah teens, for sending a message of hope rather than anger.

"Feel-good doctrine"? I ask how good those kids felt the day their friends were shot. Pretty chipper is Prager's implication. My daughter's fiancé was murdered with an ax. His death was not as clean as a bullet would have made it. I forgave the one(s) who did this to Bobby. And I'll tell any of you who feel as Mr. Prager, I didn't forgive him because it *felt good.* I forgave him because that is what Jesus would do. I forgave him in spite of my initial desire that the murderer get what he deserve. It is not easy to exchange hate for compassion.

Mercy is loving the enemy and wanting to make a positive difference. Mercy is more than I can do on my own. A source of power beyond myself is needed in order for me to deliver forgiveness and love to an enemy. And often my stomach feels sick all the while. It isn't a matter of *feeling good;* it's a decision to stop the destruction of a society that is coming unraveled.

Mercy is not easily digested, and many back away from it because they have misgivings about its appropriateness. Let's examine some of these misgivings.

Why Should *We* Have to Take on the Task of Reconciliation?

God is obsessed with the restoration of relationships—him to us, us to him, and us to us—and mercy is often the only way to effect restoration. God works hard to see that restoration happens. He asks us to cancel worship so we can be united in spirit; he asks us to leave our gifts at the altar and be reconciled (see Matt. 5:23–24). He asks us to show kindness many times to the same undeserving offender (see Matt. 18:22).

Relationship with us is so important to God that he allowed his sinless, perfect Son to take on our sin—to become sin—in order to remove the barrier that separated us from him. "God made him who had no sin to be sin for us, so that in him we might become the righteousness of God" (2 Cor. 5:21). For the self-righteous (not the snob, now, but any who try to work their way into his good graces), this passage means little. To those of us who finally admit our personal and outrageous decay, this verse is a miracle.

God made Jesus become every sin throughout the ages—mine and yours included. So terrible was this transference of sin that daylight turned to darkness for three hours while Jesus hung on the cross. The Father allowed Jesus to become sin so that "we might become the righteousness of God." There was no other way to accomplish reconciliation. None.

In light of God's great sacrifice, how can we have misgivings about extending mercy in order to restore relationships? Along with the new sinless identity afforded to us by Christ's death, we are to see others in a new light as well: "From now on we regard no one from a worldly point of view. Though we once regarded Christ in this way, we do so no longer. Therefore, if anyone is in Christ, he is a new creation; the old has gone, the new has come!" (2 Cor. 5:16–17). Of these new things, mercy is one.

We, alongside Christ, have now been given the ministry of reconciling relationships: "All this is from God, who reconciled us to himself through Christ and gave us the ministry of reconciliation: that God was reconciling the world to himself in Christ, not counting men's sins against them. And he has committed to us the message of reconciliation" (2 Cor. 5:18–19).

What an awesome task we have been given, and what a significant role mercy plays in carrying out this task. What is the key to reconciliation in the passage above? It is "not counting men's sins against them." I see no other way to put marriages, churches, or communities back together. No other way is specified. The entire process of putting lives back together revolves around "not counting men's sins against them." Jesus taught it and lived it—even while being crucified. Stephen did the same.

Based on the percentage of unbelievers, Jesus' attempt at reconciliation has failed more times than it has succeeded. Yet it is God's will that we, too, make efforts at reconciliation—even if our efforts are rejected. Our attempts at reconciliation may even lead to unjust suffering—as they did for Christ. But we have been called to follow in the footsteps of Jesus' suffering: "If you suffer for doing good and you endure it, this is commendable before God. To this you were called, because Christ suffered for you, leaving you an example, that you should follow in his steps" (1 Pet. 2:20–21).

Aren't There Times When Mercy Is Inappropriate?

To worry over whether or not mercy should be shown is to miss the point. The issue is not guilt or innocence. Guilt is a given. The issue is that the level of mercy we extend to others determines God's mercy toward us. That is the issue. When we, with the apostle Paul, will say, "I am the worst of all sinners" (see 1 Tim. 1:15), our misgivings about extending mercy to others will evaporate. We will be able to work with others without anger and bitterness. We will adjust how we deal with others—not that we become naive, but that we become tender while we work and work and work to mend broken relationships and restore shattered lives.

I understand that mercy becomes very difficult when we face issues such as rape and abuse. We recoil in disgust and condemnation and feel certain that *those* offenses do not merit mercy. But that's the whole point. None of us merits mercy. The way we feel about the most horrible, violent offenses doesn't begin to touch how much even our own "minor" sins pain God.

When we withhold mercy and forgiveness from our own family members, the destruction inflicted at least equals, if not surpasses, the acts of violence we fear. We don't have a clue as to the damage done when Mom won't speak to Dad for a week because he didn't put gasoline in the car. And children watch and learn that this is the way married people act.

We have no understanding of the harm done when unforgiving, unyielding, disgruntled church members march out of churches because they can't get their way. And children watch and learn that walking away is the solution to problems. Then when those children grow up and walk away from their marriages or their problems, they can't understand why their parents object. They're doing just as they've been trained: Withhold affection when you feel slighted; walk away and find something more suitable. Our inattention to the miracle of mercy is just as big a threat to our families as the possible threats of physical violence and harm.

Alan Redpath brings a solid and important question to the table.

> Tell me this—has the Lord ever looked into your heart? He looked Peter through and through; He searched out the rich young ruler and scores of others. Have you ever allowed Jesus to diagnose your case? It is amazing how we Christians can hide behind our creed and our doctrine and our belief in the Bible and allow ourselves to become hard and cynical so that the task that should be so tender has become cankerous.[1]

If we have misgivings about offering mercy to others, we have yet to discover ourselves in the pigpen hungering for the husks left by the hogs. We remain on the back porch with the elder brother—hard and cynical—pouting over the affairs of the rest of the family. Calculating how good we are and how neglected we've been, we wonder why we aren't happy.

Isn't Mercy Tantamount to Winking at Sin?

If we forgive others of their wrongs, aren't we making light of their sin? No. A thousand times no. Mercy is not the same thing as overlooking sin. On the contrary, mercy means looking sin squarely in the face and acknowledging its severity. Mercy insists upon the admission of sin. We are not to overlook sin. We are to admit our own. At this juncture, misgivings regarding mercy dissipate. The problem with most of us is that we worry about "winking" at *someone else's* sin. Mercy insists that we talk about our *own*.

Consider Nathan as he approached David considering his sin with Bathsheba. Nathan posed a question to David about how he would feel if a rich man, who had many sheep, took the only pet lamb from a poor man to feed a visitor.

> David burned with anger against the man and said to Nathan, "As surely as the Lord lives, the man who did this deserves to die! He must pay for that lamb four times over, because he did such a thing and had no pity."
>
> Then Nathan said to David, "You are the man!" (2 Sam. 12:5–7)

Pow!

Our misgivings about bestowing mercy to others are quenched when we realize, "*I* am the man!" or "*I* am the woman!" My greatest spiritual release came when I saw myself for the guilty person that I am. I finally saw that the sinner is not they, he, or she. *It is I!* If this realization is not the greatest issue in life, it must be one of the greatest.

The Word constantly reminds us of two principles regarding judgment: (1) Don't judge others, and (2) do judge yourself. We often practice the reverse. I encounter so many people whose unhappiness is matched by their accusing hearts. They, like David, can see what is wrong with all the world. But Nathan would never have a chance of convincing them of what is wrong within themselves—and they have misgivings about imparting mercy to others.

God's call from cover to cover is, "You need help! Let me help!" In the first book, when God found Adam and Eve improperly clothed and ashamed, he covered them. In the last book he said, "You say, 'I am rich; I have acquired wealth and do not need a thing.' But you do not realize that you are wretched, pitiful, poor, blind and naked" (Rev. 3:17). He invites us to bring our sin to him that we may be covered by his mercy. How dare we withhold this mercy from others?

Am I Really Expected to Be Merciful to My *Enemies?*

The fact is, those who sin against you are not the enemy. They are pawns manipulated by invisible and dark forces. God's Word is clear about this: "Our struggle is not against flesh and blood, but against the rulers, against the authorities, against the powers of this dark world and against the spiritual forces of evil in the heavenly realms" (Eph. 6:12). As much as we know God wouldn't lie to us, we struggle with blaming Satan instead of the people he uses to hurt us. We might understand this concept in our heads, but it sometimes takes awhile to reach our hearts.

It took awhile to reach mine. I've had to make a big adjustment in my willingness to be merciful to those I considered enemies. My nature would leave me on the back porch pouting that the sinner was going unpunished and, worse yet, was honored. What a ripoff! I despised sinners. Yet, I was wrong. Let me be clear, *I was very wrong.*

Have you ever found yourself so disgusted with others that you could not take the Lord's Supper because of the grief they brought your heart? Me, too . . . until. Listen to 1 Corinthians 11:28: "A man ought to examine *himself* before he eats of the bread and drinks of the cup" (emphasis added). Oops! Why did Paul have to word it that way? We are to examine ourselves, not others.

Through this restructuring of my attitude, I discovered something that, at first, I didn't like. I learned that mercy is not a sleight of hand that allows sinners to justify sin; it is a call to admit *my* sin. I'm to remove the plank out of my own eye. Once I do, I'll not deny the sin of another. I will notice, though, that my vision has been blurred. Compared to the plank in my own eye, theirs is just a speck. My misgivings about being generous with mercy were resolved when I accepted the truth that *I* am guilty. Never before had I seen the enormity of sin and my total inability to conquer it. Simultaneously, never before had I seen the magnificence of mercy and its miraculous power to heal.

Surely, There Are Limits to Mercy?

We have difficulty surrendering ourselves and our rights for the sake of another—especially a guilty other. No other theme jerks our chains or raises our dander like mercy. Mercy is insistent, as well as persistent. At each opportunity for mercy, we have a choice to make: We can allow *Jesus* to reign supreme, or we can trade in our crosses for whistles and badges and set about the task of *judging*. We can Barney Fife our way through the Christian path, blowing whistles and citing every infraction, or we can graciously acknowledge our desperate need for God's mercy and, in turn, extend it to others.

The story of Hosea is a portrayal of supreme mercy—mercy without limits. Israel's unfaithfulness to God is depicted in Hosea's wife, who left him for wicked lovers. The love and commitment that compelled Hosea to pursue his idolatrous and adulterous wife also compels our Lord in his passionate quest for his fallen children. Gomer is regarded as the prodigal wife.

George Robinson describes the high call of mercy in relation to Hosea's dealings with Gomer:

> The truest of all patriots is he who, like Hosea, identifies himself with his people, sorrows over their calamities as though they were his own, and repents for their sins as though he had committed them himself.[2]

The implications of the story of Hosea are mind-boggling. If we are to be like Hosea, we will actually (1) identify with the sins or our enemies, (2) sorrow over the calamities they bring upon themselves, and (3) repent for their sins as if they are our own. This is mercy without limits. This is the kind of mercy we want from God, and this is the kind of mercy he asks us to give to others.

Jesus' Answer to Our Misgivings

While Jesus was here on earth, many expressed misgivings about mercy. When he forgave the sins of the paralytic who was let down through a roof, the religious observers objected: Who does this guy think he is? He thinks he can forgive sins. Where does he get off spouting out this forgiveness stuff? (see Luke 5:21).

Twice in the book of Matthew, Jesus makes a defense for being merciful to the "bums of society." "It is not the healthy who need a doctor, but the sick. But go and learn what this means: 'I desire mercy, not sacrifice.' For I have not come to call the righteous, but sinners" (9:12–13). Again in chapter 12, "If you had known what these words mean, 'I desire mercy, not sacrifice,' you would not have condemned the innocent" (v. 7).

Ultimately, Jesus' answer to our misgivings about mercy was his death on the cross. His death said that *I* am the one in need of mercy. *I* am the sick one. And his death says that if he was willing to extend mercy to other sinners, then surely I must be willing to do the same.

The magnificent miracle of mercy puts a crack in our humanistic foundation. It is totally inconsistent with the philosophy that calls for "an eye for an eye and tooth for a tooth." It is beyond and greater than human scholarship or self-righteous spirituality. We are reminded again and again that "judgment without mercy will be shown to anyone who has not been merciful. Mercy triumphs over judgment!" (James 2:13).

May we overcome our misgivings about mercy as we realize that mercy is the way of God. Yes, it is extravagant. Yes, it is totally undeserved. That is the nature of God and the nature of mercy.

the message of MERCY

CHAPTER 12

I tell you: Love your enemies and pray for those who persecute you, that you may be sons of your Father in heaven.

—Matthew 5:44–45

12

the
message
of
MERCY

Mercy is the toughest love. We tire of dealing with the crippled and retarded actions of others. So we change residences, change jobs, change mates, change friends, change to an unlisted number—anything to lock out and cast away the very ones God commands us to accept. Yes. Mercy is tough. Mercy is the message of God not because it *works* but because it is his *nature*.

We are not guaranteed that our efforts at reconciliation will work out. Our commitment to act mercifully cannot hinge on a positive response from the other person. Mercy resembles faith in that its fruit is only evident after we make the first move. Mercy is to be our nature because it is the style of the Lamb of God.

Stanley Hauerwas and William Willimon make this observation about the Sermon on the Mount.

> The basis for the ethics of the Sermon on the Mount is not what works but rather the way God is. Cheek-turning is not advocated as what works (it usually does not), but advocated because this is the way God is—God is kind to the ungrateful and the self-ish. This is not a stratagem for getting what we want but the only manner of life available, now that, in Jesus, we have seen what God wants. We seek reconciliation with the neighbor, not because we will feel so much better afterward, but because reconciliation is what God is doing in the world in the Christ. The whole Sermon is not about how to be better individual Christians, it is a picture of the way the church is to look.[1]

When life gets complicated, I often hear people say, "God just wants me to be happy," or "They deserve some happiness after all they've been through." Find that in Scripture. It is not there. Such comments are often offered from the best intentions. But the ways of the Kingdom are often the opposite of the ways of the world. Yes, joy and blessings are found in the midst of pain and struggle, but living a life of mercy does not always make us happy. We are to choose this way because it is the way of God.

The message of mercy brings fulfillment beyond our wildest dreams, but its message leads us in the footsteps of Jesus—and that path is not always smooth. Philippians 1 calls believers to suffer conflict, and chapter 3 calls us to fellowship with Christ in his sufferings. This life isn't our happy hunting ground. It is our test for entry into the endless world of his presence.

Mercy Creates a New Identity

One of the most astounding messages of mercy is that forgiveness gives the sinner a new identity. When you forgive others, you actually free your enemies from their identity as people who hurt you and change it to that of people who need you. Hear what Philip Yancey has to say on this matter:

> When you forgive someone, you slice away the wrong from the person who did it. You disengage that person from his hurtful act. You recreate him. At one moment you identify him ineradicably as the person who did you wrong. The next moment you change that identity. He is remade in your memory.

You think of him now not as the person who hurt you, but as a person who needs you. You feel him now not as the person who alienated you, but as the person who belongs to you. Once you branded him as a person powerful in evil, but now you see him as a person weak in his needs. You recreated your past by recreating the person whose wrong made your past painful.[2]

Could this be the reason God has so much to say about new birth, new start, and new life? Surely. Mercy plays a significant role in the great miracle of renewal. "From now on we regard no one from a worldly point of view. Though we once regarded Christ in this way, we do so no longer. Therefore, if anyone is in Christ, he is a new creation; the old has gone, the new has come!" (2 Cor. 5:16–17).

In 1997, ABC's *Good Morning America* interviewed a young woman declared guilty of manslaughter due to drunk driving. Other guests included the slain man's parents and the judge of the case. The story was one of mercy. When the jury declared her guilty, the parents approached the judge and asked that she not serve time in prison. Their reasoning was that it would not bring back their son. They preferred that his untimely death be useful, fruitful.

Today this woman travels to high schools and campuses, at the recommendation of the forgiving couple, and warns students of the disasters of drinking and driving. The program is a huge success. When asked if he'd received strong opposition for allowing the guilty woman to go free, the judge said, "Yes. And if I had it to do all over, I'd do it again and a thousand more just like it. It is one of the few times I've seen justice work this well."

The message of mercy rings loud and clear in true stories like this one where mercy overcame judgment and bestowed a new identity on a devastated person.

Mercy is evidenced by God's ability to change people on any given day. How much bitterness festers over past struggles that have been repented of and apologized for? We are called to see others as new day by day. In 1 Peter 1:3, Peter says that God's mercy allows us to start life over, to be born again. What does our mercy do for others, if not the same?

Mercy Frees Us from the Worry That We Have Been Sinned Against

My observation is that we choose to live in absolute sadness because we have been sinned against. We know the difference between right and wrong, and we are sure of one fact: We have been wronged.

When someone sins against us, we are tempted to abandon our ministry of mercy. All of a sudden the possibility of granting spiritual renewal to another loses its appeal. Our power to lift the weight of another's sin is traded for the glee of taking the proverbial pound of flesh. This is a dark, ungodly, and ruthless mistake.

Hebrews 2 reminds us that Jesus came over to the sinners' side in order to become a merciful and faithful high priest (vv. 14–18). I'm afraid some of us don't like the theme of mercy because our anger against the sinner is stronger than our commitment to the Savior.

I can hear his Irish accent as my dear, dear (pronounced "dare, dare") friend Jim McGuiggan writes about our struggle to apply mercy to the sins of others.

> Believe me when I tell you that I'm not interested in minimizing sin—not yours or mine. I know all the verses, I have some idea of what the Cross of Christ says about our sin, and I can become as infuriated as the next person when someone undoubtedly guilty seems to get away with something. When it comes to sin, I know it's important that we take God's side even against ourselves.
>
> None of that is especially noble or profound.

We all feel this way, don't we? We don't want our sin whitewashed.

But the Cross must be allowed its full implications. God knew us to be sinners from the beginning; no one needed to lecture him about our evil. He alone in all the universe takes it with the utmost seriousness—and still he loves us. The Cross didn't create the love of God for sinners; it manifested it, made it known in a way that defies full comprehension.

However maddening our own sin or the sin of others is to us, we aren't given permission to make sin say more than the Cross! The Cross speaks louder than sin! Where sin shouts, the Cross thunders; where evil increases, grace in the Cross increases more and deals with it all; where sin whispers its lies and confuses us, the Cross heralds its truth and drives away the darkness.

God pities us! He sees us as not only sinners but as sinned against. He has a heart full of compassion, a heart eager beyond words to forgive us. We mustn't keep that truth from people, no matter what evil they've done.[3]

When we see what God sees—sinners who are sinned against—our sense of mercy ought to vault to the surface.

God didn't just save sinners; he saved sinners from other sinners. We aren't the only ones being offended; our offenders are simultaneously offended. That is why revenge never works. The layers of offense run too deep. We can't afford not to forgive others. Rather, we must seek ways to justify our enemies, for while they are the offenders in our lives, we may be the offenders in theirs. And even if we are not their offenders, others are!

Lewis Smedes makes a stunning observation about how God applies mercy. "First, God rediscovers the humanity of the person who wronged him, by removing the barrier created by sin. Second, God surrenders his right to get even, choosing instead to bear the cost in his own body. Finally, God revises his feelings toward us, finding a way to 'justify' us so that when he looks upon us he sees his own adopted children, with his divine image restored."[4]

If we can but keep the message of the Cross forefront in our minds and remember, as Jim McGuiggan said, that the Cross shouts louder than sin, we, with God, will have hearts full of compassion and love for those who sin against us.

Mercy Gives Us Opportunity to Commune with God

It is when we learn to take up the Cross of Christ daily that we genuinely become one with him, as we fellowship his sufferings. E. Stanley Jones notes, "But man is invited to be like God in self-surrender. And when he does he finds himself, not as God, but in communion with God at God's highest point, self-surrender."[5] The message of mercy is that we are honored to commune with the Living One when we mercifully and faithfully yield to another.

In *Mind of Jesus,* William Barclay writes that the way to deal with sin is simply through Jesus.

> One of the great effects of sin is the disturbance of personal relationships; one of the great effects of the work of Christ is the creation of fellowship. It is only in Christ that men can find unity instead of disunity, trust instead of suspicion, love instead of hate. The mutual hostility which is created by sin is defeated by the love which is shed abroad by Christ. It enables us to deal with the situation which sin had created "between us and God." The work of Christ assures us of the love and of the forgiveness of God, and our desire to hide from God is changed into a great desire to live for ever with God.
>
> The work of Christ is effective, first, in revealing to us the love of God, and, second, in enabling us by his risen power to deal with the tragic and disastrous situations which sin had created in our own lives and in the life of the world.

No man can ever grasp, still less express, all that Jesus Christ has done, but we may be well content to witness with all our hearts that through Jesus Christ we have entered into a relationship with God, which without him would have been utterly impossible, and in him we have entered into a relationship with ourselves and with our fellowmen in which the deadly work of sin can be undone.[6]

Sin is deadly and disastrous; it is worse than the mind can imagine. And the undoing of this tragedy is found only in Jesus. Nowhere else . . . ever. When we respond to the wrongs of others with Christlike love and forgiveness, we will find ourselves in communion with God.

Mercy Is about Going the Extra Mile

Hear Jesus. Go the extra mile—not for your friend but for your antagonistic, obnoxious competitor. "If someone forces you to go one mile, go with him two miles" (Matt. 5:41). Do it for the very one who just walked out on you. Give them something—other than a piece of your mind. If your departing friend or spouse takes your stereo to his or her new apartment—equipped with one set of keys and a

restraining order—give the departee the TV as well. "If someone wants to sue you and take your tunic, let him have your cloak as well" (Matt. 5:40).

It may need to be said that there are times when corrective measures are appropriate. Repentance is required. But most people don't really want a system of total justice— where every sin is met with fair and just consequences, where restitution is required for every offense. All of us would be lost under such a system. This is the "eye for an eye and a tooth for a tooth" system that Jesus came to overturn by his death on the cross. Mercy from the Cross of Christ is the only way out. And it is our only way in . . . to heaven.

Do you know of a church with a strong, well-known doctrine that insists its members go the extra mile for the enemy in order to be children of God? Neither do I. How quickly we brush past this phrase: "that you may be sons of your Father in heaven" (Matt. 5:45). We are too busy trying to decide whether we should hail Mary, tithe before or after taxes, or allow mixed swimming at church camp to hear the voice of Jesus whisper, "You must care for those who abuse you in order to be classified as my brother and my Father's child."

Mercy's Perfection Is Love

When Jesus called us to perfection in Matthew 5, he was not calling us to sinlessness but to love.

> Love your enemies and pray for those who persecute you, that you may be sons of your Father in heaven. . . . If you love those who love you, what reward will you get? Are not even the tax collectors doing that? And if you greet only your brothers, what are you doing more than others? Do not even the pagans do that? Be perfect, therefore, as your heavenly Father is perfect. (vv. 44–48)

In this passage, Jesus challenges us to love our enemies. He reminds us that it is not noteworthy when we love those who love us; rather, perfection is attained when we love those who hate us. How different is this perfection from earthly minded perfection? Those who call for perfection in the lives of others have no taste for God's type of perfection. They want the flesh to shape up, yet they care nothing for the inner life. God calls us to perfect what lies below the surface.

And how do we cultivate this love for others? God has provided. We can love as the Father loves because the Holy Spirit has been poured out in our hearts, growing the fruit

of kindness, gentleness, and patience in us. We can *choose* perfection.

Mercy Forgives Seventy Times Seven

"Then Peter came and said to Him, 'Lord, how often shall my brother sin against me and I forgive him? Up to seven times?' Jesus said to him, 'I do not say to you, up to seven times, but up to seventy times seven'" (Matt. 18:21–22 NASB). If you think the question "Up to seven times?" is silly, think how you react when you are required to forgive a repeated error just three times. Not only is it difficult, but it also gets old. To forgive up to seven times is out of the question for most of us. We begin to "beg off" in order to justify our lack of spiritual commitment and maturity. We invent little phrases that sound good to the flesh-mind, like, "I don't want to be an enabler."

So when Jesus answered with the specific "up to seventy times seven," he was identifying with our human flesh in a concrete way that we could understand. Mercy does not deny the carnage of sin; it does something about it. It asks us to forgive.

But Jesus never asks us to do something that he hasn't already done himself: "You see, at just the right time, when we were still powerless, Christ died for the ungodly. . . .

God demonstrates his own love for us in this: While we were still sinners, Christ died for us" (Rom. 5:6, 8). This is mercy! We are called to die on our crosses daily for the same sort that Jesus died for . . . sinners just like us.

Mercy Deals Gently with Weakness

The message of mercy, finally, is that we deal with one another mindful that we are weak creatures. We cannot, on our own, repair the destruction to our souls. Only the miracle of mercy is sufficient to restore us.

The psalmist depicts our Lord's gentle dealing:

> The Lord is compassionate and gracious, slow to anger, abounding in love. He will not always accuse, nor will he harbor his anger forever; he does not treat us as our sins deserve or repay us according to our iniquities. For as high as the heavens are above the earth, so great is his love for those who fear him; as far as the east is from the west, so far has he removed our transgressions from us. As a father has compassion on his children, so the Lord has compassion on those who fear him; for he knows how we are formed, he remembers that we are dust. (Ps. 103:8–14)

Before anyone tries to label the miracle of mercy as too easy, too lenient, let me stop such lunacy. Mercy is God's message. Mercy requires sobriety, commitment, and strength. The silly and the glib will not like mercy—mercy is tough. May I remind you that the one who calls for the miracle of mercy is the only one who sweat blood and shed blood . . . so that we could receive mercy.

Mercy? It is as indescribable and as eternal as God. We will receive it only if we choose to practice it as God does . . . in the most hostile terrains. May his mercy be waiting for us when we arrive on the Big Day. May we be quick to repent of the sin of being unmerciful. *God, please give us this miracle.*

NOTES

Chapter One. The Marvel of Mercy

1. Philip Yancey, *What's So Amazing about Grace?* (Grand Rapids, Mich.: Zondervan Publishing House, 1997), 98.

2. Ibid.

3. William Backus and Marie Chapian, *Telling Yourself the Truth* (Minneapolis, Minn.: Bethany House, 1980), 21.

4. Stanley Hauerwas and William Willimon, *Resident Aliens: Life in the Christian Colony* (Nashville, Tenn.: Abingdon Press, 1989), 91.

5. William Willimon, *The Intrusive Word: Preaching to the Unbaptized* (Grand Rapids, Mich.: Wm. B. Eerdmans Publishing, 1994), 74–77.

6. Brennan Manning, *The Signature of Jesus* (Old Tappan, N.J.: Chosen Books, 1988), 19.

Chapter Two. The Mystery of Mercy

1. Willimon, *Intrusive Word,* 22–23.
2. Manning, *The Ragamuffin Gospel: Embracing the Unconditional Love of God* (Portland, Ore.: Multnomah, 1990), 16.

Chapter Three. The Mandate of Mercy

1. Michael Wells, *Sidetracked in the Wilderness* (Tarrytown, N.Y.: Fleming H. Revell, 1991), 28.

Chapter Five. The Master of Mercy

1. Manning, *Ragamuffin Gospel,* 89.
2. J. I. Packer, *Knowing God* (Downers Grove, Ill.: Inter-Varsity Press, 1973), 78.
3. Henri Nouwen, *In the Name of Jesus: Reflections on Christian Leadership* (New York: Crossroad, 1996), 65–66.
4. Wells, *Sidetracked in the Wilderness,* 137.
5. Erma Bombeck, *If I Had My Life to Live Over Again.*
6. Manning, *Ragamuffin Gospel,* 102.

Chapter Six. The Menace of Mercy

1. Yancey, *What's So Amazing about Grace?*, 181.

2. Rebecca Pippert, *A Heart Like His: The Shaping of Character in the Choices of Life* (Wheaton, Ill.: Crossway Books, 1996), 14.

3. Jim Cymbala, *Fresh Wind, Fresh Fire: What Happens When God's Spirit Invades the Heart of His People* (Grand Rapids, Mich.: Zondervan Publishing House, 1997), 118.

4. Oswald Chambers, *Not Knowing Where* (Grand Rapids, Mich.: Discovery House, 1989), 25.

5. Ibid., 33.

6. Paul Tournier, *Guilt and Grace* (New York: Harper and Row, 1962), 85.

7. Chuck Colson, *Who Speaks for God?* (Manchester, Ill.: Rossway Books, 1985), 136.

8. Chambers, *Not Knowing Where,* 186.

9. Yancey, *What's So Amazing about Grace?*, 198.

Chapter Seven. The Miracle of Mercy

1. Pippert, *Heart Like His,* 93–95.

Chapter Eight. The Might of Mercy

1. Eugene Peterson, *Leap over a Wall: Earthy Spirituality*

for Everyday Christians (San Francisco: HarperCollins, 1997), 101.

2. Charles Stanley, *The Blessings of Brokenness: Why God Allows Us to Go through Hard Times* (Grand Rapids, Mich.: Zondervan Publishing House, 1997), 132.

3. Manning, *Signature of Jesus,* 124.

4. Andrew Murray, *Day by Day* (Minneapolis, Minn.: Bethany House, 1961), 79.

5. Denny Gunderson, *Through the Dust: Servant Leadership Using Jesus As an Example* (Franklin, Tenn.: YWAM, 1992), 100.

6. Pippert, *Heart Like His,* 83.

Chapter Nine. The Measure of Mercy

1. Wells, *Sidetracked in the Wilderness,* 12.

2. Yancey, *What's So Amazing about Grace?,* 64.

3. Fenelon, *The Seeking Heart* (Auburn, Maine: The Seedsowers Christian Books Publishing House, 1992), 47.

4. Willimon, *Intrusive Word,* 60.

5. Adrian Rogers, *Believe in Miracles, but Trust in Jesus* (Wheaton, Ill.: Crossway Books, 1997), 155.

Chapter Ten. The Methods of Mercy

1. Rogers, *Believe in Miracles,* 141.

2. Fenelon, *Seeking Heart,* 41–42.

3. Wells, *Sidetracked in the Wilderness,* 64.

4. Yancey, *What's So Amazing about Grace?,* 61.

5. Jim McGuiggan, *Jesus, Hero of Thy Soul* (West Monroe, La.: Howard Publishing, 1998), 173.

6. E. Stanley Jones, *The Divine Yes* (Nashville, Tenn.: Abingdon Press, 1992), 109.

Chapter Eleven. The Misgivings of Mercy

1. Alan Redpath, *Victorious Christian Living: Studies in the Book of Joshua* (Grand Rapids, Mich.: Revell, 1993), 50.

2. George L. Robinson, *Twelve Minor Prophets* (Grand Rapids, Mich.: Baker, 1926), 26.

Chapter Twelve. The Message of Mercy

1. Hauerwas and Willimon, *Resident Aliens,* 85.

2. Yancey, *What's So Amazing about Grace?,* 102–3.

3. McGuiggan, *Jesus, Hero of Thy Soul,* 175–76.

4. Yancey, *What's So Amazing about Grace?,* 106.

5. Jones, *Victory through Surrender: Self-Realization through Self-Surrender* (Nashville, Tenn.: Festival, 1966), 68.

6. William Barclay, *Mind of Jesus* (New York: Harper and Row, 1976), 286.

Printed in the United States
By Bookmasters